The Craps Answer Book

The Craps Answer Book

How to Make One of the Best Bets

in the Casino Even Better

John Grochowski

Bonus Books, Inc.
Chicago, Illinois

05   04   03   02   01   5   4   3   2   1

Library of Congress Control Number

ISBN 1-56625-169-9

Bonus Books, Inc.
160 E. Illinois St.
Chicago, IL 60611

Printed in the United States of America

Contents

	Introduction	xi
Pass No. 1	Getting Started	1
	Answers	5
Pass No. 2	Definitions	11
	Answers	13
Pass No. 3	Odds and Edges	23
	Answers	27
Pass No. 4	The Match Game	35
	Answers	39
Pass No. 5	On the Line	43
	Answers	49
Pass No. 6	Place or Buy	63
	Answers	67
Pass No. 7	The Bad and the Ugly	73
	Answers	77
Pass No. 8	Getting Edgy	85
	Answers	89
Pass No. 9	A Systems Sampler	93
	Answers	97
Pass No. 10	The Readers Write	113
	Answers	117

Introduction

Many years ago, before my wife Marcy and I were about to take our first trip to Las Vegas, her brother was giving us the inside dope of what we should do.

"Craps is the best game," he told us. "There's nothing like it. You want to bet on the pass line. Here's what you do . . ."

With that, he was off on an explanation, complete with table diagrams.

I have to admit, my eyes glazed over. I was ready to be pointed toward a blackjack table, a slot machine . . . anything to avoid this hopelessly complicated game.

It was a year later, before our second Vegas venture, that I actually learned to play. I did it by practicing at home, looking at the rules in a book as I played out imaginary pass line bets.

Along the way, I discovered what I hope others will discover in this book. Craps isn't a difficult game at all. Casino games aren't designed to intimidate players. They're designed to AT-TRACT players. And while craps may be an acquired taste, once players get used to a few ins and outs, they become fanatics. The craps table is among the most exciting spots in the casino. When you hear a big group cheer in the casino, it's undoubtedly coming from a craps table. There's a camaraderie among players winning and losing together that can't be matched at any other game.

Many years after those first casino vacations, when I started writing a gaming column for the *Chicago Sun-Times*, I discovered that my early trepidations about craps were not at all unusual. Not a month has passed since the column first appeared in February 1994, that someone hasn't written to tell me they just don't understand craps. In fact, early in the process of writing this book, I received an e-mail from a woman who was taking her father to the casino, and they just hadn't been able to figure out how to play. I wrote back, walking her step-by-step through the process of betting on the pass line, suggesting that they get a pair of dice and practice at home. She wrote back later. It had all clicked. Now they had a starting point.

That starting point, the pass line, is one of the best bets in the casino, and if my correspondent and her father never learn anything else about the game, they can have fun and give themselves a better shot to win than most of the players in the casino.

Potential players often are attracted by the excitement of the craps table, but then are scared off by the enormous number of betting options. It all looks so confusing. But what confuses the issue is that there are many, many bad bets at the table. The game is simplified immensely when players ignore most of the betting options, and focus in on the few that give them the best shots to win.

I aim to help you focus on those best bets, and tune out the bad ones. I also aim to make all this painless, even fun, for those of you who think you just can't understand craps. Along the way, we'll look through some trivia, history and fun facts about craps and dice games. We'll also take a glance at systems play and how systems work—or don't work—without dwelling too heavily on specific systems.

Do as that woman who e-mailed did with her dad: Check out the explanations, and practice with a pair of dice at home before heading for the tables. Before going to the casino, you should have a solid plan of attack based on bets with the lowest house edge possible.

ANSWER BOOKS

This is the fourth in my series of Answer Books for Bonus Books in Chicago, following *The Casino Answer Book*, *The Slot Machine Answer Book* and *The Video Poker Answer Book*. They are set up as quizzes, with sets of questions first and answers on the following pages. I've heard from many readers who enjoy taking the quizzes, trying to puzzle out the answers themselves before going on to the essay-style answers. However, if you want to go straight to the meat of a chapter, you can go directly to the answers without turning back to the questions. The question is repeated at the start of each answer.

The Answer Books are browsers' books. If what you really want is a discussion on whether one-roll propositions are worthwhile, then skip right on ahead to "Pass No. 7: The Bad and the Ugly" and come on back to "The Match Game" on stickmen's calls whenever you feel like it. I'd strongly suggest to new players that they focus on the good percentage bets detailed in "Pass No. 5: On the Line" and "Pass No. 6: Place or Buy." Have the good well ingrained before you worry about the bad and the ugly.

Above all, good luck when you try your hand in the casinos. Here's hoping for a hot roll coming your way soon.

Pass No. 1: Getting Started

People have been playing games of chance with dice for centuries, even millennia. Craps itself is derived from games that predate settlement of the Americas. Let's warm up with a few odds and ends about craps and dice games.

1. **The earliest regularly shaped dice have been found in:**

    A. England, from the time of King Arthur
    B. France, from the time of Charlemagne
    C. Ancient Rome, from the time of the early Caesars
    D. Late Stone Age Iraq

2. **Dice have been found that were made from:**

    A. Wood
    B. Bone
    C. Clay
    D. Stone
    E. All of the above
    F. None of the above

3. **A die has been found in an ancient Roman site that is unusual in that:**

    A. It has 12 sides
    B. It is the earliest die made of plastic
    C. It has no spots
    D. It has four spots on two different faces

4. The modern six-sided dice used in casinos are made of:

    A. Ivory

    B. Plexiglas

    C. Cellulose

    D. Amber

5. Each edge of a casino die measures:

    A. One inch

    B. Three-quarters of an inch

    C. Five-eighths of an inch

    D. One-half inch

6. Casino dice:

    A. Have straight edges and sharp corners

    B. Are transparent

    C. Have serial numbers

    D. All of the above

    E. None of the above

7. Opposite sides of dice should:

    A. Have consecutive numbers

    B. Add up to 7

    C. Add up to even numbers

    D. Have a difference of 2 when the smaller is subtracted from the larger

8. A modern dice game that can trace its roots to ancient Egypt of 2600 B.C. or earlier is:

    A. Backgammon

    B. Yahtzee

    C. Hazard

    D. Monopoly

9. Craps was first played by:

    A. The British in the 1100s

    B. The Portuguese in the 1500s

    C. The French in the 1700s

    D. Americans in the 1800s

10. Craps was derived from an earlier game called:

    A. Roly-poly

    B. Hazard

    C. Vingt-et-un

    D. Chinese checkers

11. The name craps comes from the French slang "krabs,", which meant:

    A. A pair of ones

    B. Dice made from crustacean shells

    C. Irritable players

    D. Baby needs a new pair of shoes

12. In modern craps, the name refers to:

    A. Losing rolls

    B. Winning rolls

    C. Irritable pit bosses

    D. A roll of 2, 3 or 12

13. The game of craps we play in casinos is more specifically called:

    A. American craps

    B. Federation craps

    C. Bank craps

    D. Craps-Hazard

14. Among table games in American casinos, the popularity of craps ranks:

    A. First

    B. Second to blackjack

    C. Third, behind blackjack and roulette

    D. Fourth, behind blackjack, roulette and Caribbean Stud

15. Among the most popular table games in American casinos, including craps, blackjack, baccarat, roulette and Caribbean Stud, the house edge at craps:

    A. Is about average

    B. Is the highest

    C. Is the lowest

    D. Can range from highest to lowest . . . so choose your bet wisely

Pass No. 1: Getting Started Answers

1. The earliest regularly shaped dice have been found in:

   D. Late Stone Age Iraq

   Dice dating to about 3000 B.C. made of baked clay, with regular sides, have been found in northern Iraq. Even older dice have been found in the Middle East, but not with sides all of the same shape and size. That, of course, would be an issue in a casino environment where an irregular shape would make some sides more likely to land face up than others.

2. Dice have been found that were made from:

   E. All of the above

   Not only have dice been found that are made from wood, clay, bone or stone, but also from peach pits, animal horns, teeth, ivory, bronze, porcelain, even jewels. Basically any material that is sturdy enough to stand up to repeated rolls has been shaped into dice.

   The slang expression "rolling the bones" has an origin that is quite literal. Dice were carved from bones for thousands of years. It was not at all unusual in Roman times, for instance, for dice to be fashioned from sheep's knuckles.

   Speaking of Roman times, one of the most famous quotes in history includes a reference to dice. In 49 B.C., when Julius Caesar and his legion crossed the Rubicon from Gaul into the Roman homeland to challenge Pompeius, Caesar said, "*Iacta alea est*," which translates into "The die is cast." ("Die" is the singular form of dice, even though craps players and crew alike often will refer to one "dice.") Caesar was saying he had rolled the dice, and there was no turning back. For craps players, there's no turning back once the shooter has cast the dice, either.

3. A die has been found in an ancient Roman site that is unusual in that:
    D. It has four spots on two different faces

It seems even the history of cheating with dice goes back 2,000 years or more. Having the same number on two sides of a die changes the odds of any dice game dramatically.

4. The modern six-sided dice used in casinos are made of:
    C. Cellulose

Cellulose is a plastic that is drawn out in rods, with pieces then cut off to turn into dice. Spots less than 0.02 of an inch deep are drilled into the faces. They're then brushed with a paint that weighs the same as the plastic, leaving sides that weigh the same regardless of how many spots have been drilled.

5. Each edge of a casino die measures:
    B. Three-quarters of an inch

Sizes and weights of casino dice are heavily regulated in casino jurisdictions throughout the United States. Nevada, as the largest, most established gaming site, sets the tone. Manufacturers claim that the sides are within 1/10,000th of three-quarters of an inch.

6. Casino dice:
    D. All of the above

The dice in casinos have straight edges and sharp corners, are transparent and are monogrammed with serial numbers. The serial numbers are an anti-cheating device. The table crew or pit boss can check serial numbers to be sure the dice in use are ones that were assigned to that table.

7. Opposite sides of dice should:

B. Add up to 7

If a die is sitting on a table so that the number on top is 6, then the number that is face down on the table should be 1. Likewise, 4 and 3 are on opposite sides, as are 2 and 5.

The arrangement of numbers on the dice give supervisors an easy way to check that all numbers are present . . . and present only once. Hold a die so that the 1 is on top and the 2 is facing you. Rotate it backward so the 2 is on top, then when you rotate it to your left, the 3 will be on top.

At that point the 4 is on the bottom, so flip it up so the 4 is on top with the 5 facing you. The same rotation you used to see 1, 2 and 3 now will allow you to see 4, 5 and 6.

That little check becomes second nature to craps supervisors, who almost unconsciously in a second or two can tell that a die has all the numbers on the faces that it should.

8. A modern dice game that can trace its roots to ancient Egypt of 2600 B.C. or earlier is:

A. Backgammon

Backgammon is derived from a game called Senet that was played by ancient Egyptians. A painting in the tomb of Hesey from about 2600 B.C. or a little earlier shows Senet being played. Backgammon appears to be an amalgam of Senet and an Asian game called Nard. Craps doesn't go back quite that far, but it has a lengthy history of its own, as we'll see in the next answer.

9. Craps was first played by:

C. The French in the 1700s

Not only did the French adapt craps from an earlier, more complex game (see below), they brought the game to North America. Craps was being played in New Orleans at the dawn of the 1800s, before the Louisiana Purchase brought the French territory into American control.

10. Craps was derived from an earlier game called:

B. Hazard

For casino players who are intimidated by craps or think it too complex, they haven't seen anything until they've given Hazard a go. Hazard is an old English game that involves two levels called a main point and a chance point.

At the start of play, the shooter keeps rolling until he rolls a two-dice total of 5, 6, 7, 8 or 9. That becomes the main point. If he rolls the main point again on the next roll, he wins. If he rolls a 2 or a 3, he loses. If he rolls an 11, and the main point is 7 he wins, but 11 loses on all other main points. If he rolls a 12, he wins if the main point is 6 or 8 and loses if the main point is 5, 7 or 9.

Confused yet? We're just starting.

If the roll after the main point does not repeat the point, but is a 4, 5, 6, 7, 8, 9 or 10, that roll becomes the chance point. Now, no other numbers matter except the main point and the chance point. If the shooter repeats the chance point first, he wins. If he repeats the main point first, he loses.

Let's walk through a sequence. The shooter starts by rolling a 6. That's the main point, and the shooter is hoping the next roll will be a 6 or a 12. He wins on either of those rolls, but loses on 11. Instead, he rolls a 9. That becomes the chance point. The next several rolls are 5 . . . 7 . . . 11 . . . 8. None of them matter. Finally he rolls a 9, repeating the chance point and winning the bet. Had he rolled a 6, repeating the main point before the 9, he'd have lost.

The pass and come bets in craps, which many novices find confusing and which we'll explore later in this book, are essentially streamlined versions of Hazard.

Some sources date Hazard to the twelfth century, during the Crusades. Crusading knights are said to have played the game before attacking Hazarth castle in 1125.

11. The name craps comes from the French slang "krabs", which meant:

A. A pair of ones

No snake-eyes for the French who brought the game to New Orleans. To them, a 1 on each die was "krabs," giving the variation on Hazard its new name.

12. In modern craps, the name refers to:

D. A roll of 2, 3 or 12

The historical footnote that craps is derived from French slang for a pair of ones lives on today in that a pair of ones is among the rolls called craps. Any roll of 2, 3 or 12 is craps, which as we shall see is a first-roll loser for players negotiating the hazards of the pass line.

13. The game of craps we play in casinos is more specifically called:

C. Bank craps

We play bank craps in casinos because the casinos bank the game. That is, the casinos cover all bets, paying the winners and collecting from the losers. Away from the casinos, players often bet against each other instead of against the house. If a player calls out a bet on 6, for example, there's no action unless another player accepts and volunteers to cover the bet.

14. Among table games in American casinos, the popularity of craps ranks:

B. Second to blackjack

When the soldiers came home from World War II, craps was at the top of the heap in the casinos, then legal only in Nevada, but thriving in illegal joints. (The most famous probably were in Louisiana, but illegal casinos thrived just about anywhere with a large enough population base to support them.) Craps was the serviceman's game overseas. Dice are easily portable, and it was easy to get up a game at a moment's notice.

Blackjack surpassed craps in popularity in the 1960s, after Ed Thorpe's book *Beat the Dealer* drove home the point that blackjack is a beatable game for card counters. Most players can't count cards effectively, but the idea that the game is beatable was enough. Craps has been No. 2 on the table games list ever since.

15. Among the most popular table games in American casinos, including craps, blackjack, baccarat, roulette and Caribbean Stud, the house edge at craps:

> **D.** Can range from highest to lowest . . . so choose your bet wisely

Craps players who stick to pass, don't pass, come and don't come wagers face a house edge of only about 1.4 percent, meaning average expected losses in the long run are only about $1.40 per $100 wagered. Combine those bets with free odds, which have no house edge, and the combination drops to eight-tenths of a percent or less, depending on the size of the odds bets the casino accepts.

Compare those to the following house edges: Blackjack— small player edge for card counters; 0.5 percent approximate house edge against basic strategy players; 2 to 2.5 percent edge against average players. Baccarat—1.17 percent on bets on banker; 1.36 percent on player. Roulette—5.26 percent. Caribbean Stud—5.22 percent or higher depending on player skill.

The pass/odds combination measures up pretty well against those bets. But other craps bets, such as the one-roll proposition on any 7, have house edges as high as 16.67 percent. Yuck.

One of the most important things a craps player must learn is to stick to the good bets and to stay away from the bad ones. That's one of the things we'll be looking at in later chapters.

Pass No. 2: Definitions

Any casino game has a language that is all its own, and the language of craps may be the richest around. Below is a list of terms we'll be using throughout this book. For experienced players, definitions will be a snap. But for craps newcomers, let's make sure we're on the same page. Define the following:

1. **Layout**
2. **Shooter**
3. **Roll**
4. **Craps**
5. **Comeout**
6. **Pass**
7. **Don't pass**
8. **Come**
9. **Don't come**
10. **Buck**
11. **Right bettor**
12. **Wrong bettor**
13. **Place bets**
14. **Buy bets**
15. **Hard ways**

16. **Proposition bets**
17. **Lay bets**
18. **Free odds**
19. **Hedge bets**
20. **Field**
21. **Seven out**
22. **Rails**
23. **Boxman**
24. **Stickman**
25. **Dealer**

Pass No. 2: Definitions Answers

1. Layout: The felt on the table that shows all the available bets in craps. Players may put their own chips in the marked spaces on the layout to make pass, don't pass, come, don't come and field bets. For place numbers and bets marked on the center of the table, the player must slide chips toward a dealer and direct the dealer to make the bet. Players may not hand chips directly to the dealer—the folks watching in the surveillance booth want to see the transactions being made and don't want any questions of shenanigans involving palming of chips. That goes double for players just buying in. Place your cash on the layout and ask the dealer for chips.

2. Shooter: The player who is rolling the dice. All the other players at the table are betting on the shooter's rolls. The shooter keeps rolling until he sevens out (see below). Then the next player to the shooter's left is offered the chance to become the next shooter. The player can decline—you don't have to shoot if you don't want to—and players who bet against the shooter often refuse the dice.

If you do accept the dice, you must bet on the pass line. One memorable time that I refused the dice came when Harrah's in Joliet, Illinois, had unusual payoffs on the field bet that made it an even wager with no house edge. I was there to play the field and have some fun. I wasn't making any other bets, not even the pass line bets that I normally make. The shooter sevened out, and I was offered the dice. I declined, preferring to stay on the field. The player to my left then rolled five field numbers in a row, including a 2 and a 12 that each paid 3-1. I made a quick $450, and played even the rest of the day. A nice time.

Of course, things don't always work out that nicely. Another time, at the Four Queens in Las Vegas, I was playing don't pass, meaning I was betting against the shooter, and doing pretty well. I declined the dice, and the new shooter proceeded to make six passes in a row, meaning I lost six consecutive don't pass bets.

You win some, and you lose some . . .

3. Roll: This can mean a single roll of the two dice, or a whole series of rolls. Each time the shooter throws the dice it's a roll. But the shooter's entire series of rolls before sevening out is also referred to as a roll. If you're betting with the shooter, you're cheering for him to have a good, long roll. If you're betting against the shooter, you want him out of there ASAP.

4. Craps: Not just the name of the game, craps is what we call any roll of 2, 3 or 12.

5. Comeout: The first roll in a sequence that leads to a decision on pass and don't pass bets.

6. Pass: The dice are said to pass if the shooter makes his point. When that happens all players with bets on the pass line win.

Remember in Pass No. 1 how we looked at the rules of Hazard, the game from which craps is derived? The pass line bet is the wager that most closely resembles Hazard.

Here's how it works. The sequence starts with a comeout roll. If, on the comeout, the shooter rolls a 7 or 11, everyone who bets on the pass line wins. If the shooter rolls a 2, 3 or 12, everyone on the pass line loses. If the roll is 4, 5, 6, 8, 9 or 10, that becomes the point number.

When the shooter rolls a point number on the comeout, the object of the game changes. Seven is no longer a winning number—it's a loser. For pass bettors to win, the shooter must roll that number again before rolling the next 7. If the 7 shows up first, the pass bettors lose. No other numbers but the point and the 7 affect the wager.

Let's walk through a sequence. On the comeout roll, the shooter rolls a 10. That becomes the point. Subsequently, he rolls 4 . . . 2 . . . 9 . . . 6 . . . 5 . . . 8 . . . 8 again . . . 6. None of those rolls affect the pass wagers. The players' chips just stay on the table. Finally the shooter rolls a 7, and a groan goes up from the table. All the pass bettors lose.

Now, I could have written this example with the shooter rolling a 10 and a big cheer from the table as all the players win. Why use a losing roll as an example? Well, this was a real sequence, from a morning in the fall of 2000 at the Tropicana in Las Vegas. And there were plenty of cheers from the table before the disappointing finish. That's because most players don't just make a pass line bet and ignore the rolls that don't decide the bet. They also bet on other numbers, and on this day most of the table was betting on 6 and 8 in addition to the pass line. The shooter gave the people something to cheer about with two 6s and two 8s before rolling the 7.

The pass line bet, above all, seems to be the wager that confuses new players. Those who are used to winning or losing on every hand of blackjack or every spin of the roulette wheel seem to have trouble with the concept of waiting for several rolls of the dice before there's a decision. And what's with this deal of 7 being a good number for one roll, then turning into the worst number of all?

But it's really not all that difficult. If you're new to the game of craps, practice with a pair of dice at home. Pretend it's a comeout, and roll the dice. If you roll a 7 or 11 you win, if it's a 2, 3 or 12 you lose. Anything else becomes the point, and now the object is to roll the point again before the next 7.

Try it at home for a little while, and before long it'll become second nature. Is it worth the effort? Yep. As we'll see, this is one of the best bets in the casino. There are easier bets at the craps table, but most of them are far worse for the player.

The pass line wager is a bet you make yourself by placing chips directly in front of you in the bar marked "pass line" that runs all around the table.

7. Don't pass: Don't pass is the near opposite of pass. Players who bet on don't pass are betting against the shooter instead of with him.

On the comeout roll, 7 and 11 are losing numbers for the don't pass bettor, while 2 and 3 are winners. The 12, which is a winner for pass bettors, is just a push on don't pass—the bet is returned to the player and no money changes hands.

When the shooter rolls a point number on the comeout, the don't bettor starts hoping for a 7. If the shooter repeats the point before rolling a 7, pass bettors win and don't pass bettors lose. If he rolls the 7 first, don't pass bettors win and pass bettors lose.

Several times over the years, I've had players come to me with a system they think they've just thought up. If pass and don't pass are opposites, why not have two partners at the same table, one betting pass and the other betting don't pass? Wouldn't their wins and losses cancel each other out? They wouldn't win any money, but they could play for free and take any free drinks, meals and other comps that come their way.

Problem is, pass and don't pass aren't exact opposites. There's the sticky matter of that 12. When the shooter rolls a 12 on the comeout, the pass bettor loses, but the don't pass bettor doesn't win. He just pushes. Overall, pass and don't pass bettors lose as much in the long run as they would if they were playing identically at separate tables.

As with the pass line bet, you can make don't pass wagers yourself by placing chips in the area marked "don't pass bar."

8. Come: The come bet works the same way as the pass line bet; it's just made at a different point. If the upcoming roll is not a comeout and you want to make the equivalent of a pass line bet, wager on come instead. The next roll becomes the equivalent of a comeout roll for your come bet. If the roll is 7 or 11, you win, if it's 2, 3 or 12 you lose, and if it's anything else it becomes your come point. If the shooter repeats that number before the next 7 you win, and if a 7 comes first you lose.

Let's walk through a sequence. On the comeout roll, the shooter rolls a 6 that becomes the point number for pass line bettors. Before the next roll, you bet on come. The shooter rolls an 8. That doesn't affect the pass line bets, but it becomes your point number on the come. The next rolls are 4 . . . 9 . . . 5 . . . 2 . . . 11 . . . 10. None of them make any difference to either the pass bet or the come bet. Finally, the shooter rolls an 8. Your come bet wins, and the pass bettors are still in action, waiting for either a 6 or a 7 to decide the bet.

What if instead of the second 8 the shooter had rolled a 7? Then both the pass and come bettors would have lost since the 7 would have come before either the 6 that was the point on the pass line or the 8 that was the point on the come bet.

This is another bet you can make yourself, by placing chips in the large area marked "come" just beyond the pass line.

9. Don't come: Just as the come bet works the same way as the pass line bet, the don't come bet works the same way as the don't pass bet. The only difference is that you make the don't come bet on rolls that aren't comeouts for pass or don't pass wagers.

You can wager on don't come by placing chips in the area marked "don't come." It's much smaller than the come area, because there are many fewer players that bet on don't come.

10. Buck: Players just coming up to the table don't have to ask if the next roll is a comeout. They can tell at a glance by looking for the buck, a black-and-white disc that says "Off" on one side and "On" on the other. If the next roll is a comeout, the buck will be turned to the "Off" side and will be in the don't come area on a corner of the layout. If it is not a comeout roll and a point number already has been established, the buck will be turned to "On" and be sitting in a numbered box corresponding to the point.

11. Right bettor: Those who are betting with the shooter are said to be right bettors. They're the large majority of players, the ones who let out loud cheers whenever the shooter makes his point, rolls a winner on the place bets or just about any number but the 7 that wipes out most bets on rolls other than the come-out. It's fun to be pulling together, rooting for the shooter, enjoying wins for the whole table and groaning together over the losses. There's a camaraderie that makes craps the most social of casino games.

12. Wrong bettor: There's nothing wrong with betting against the shooter, but those who do are said to be wrong bettors nonetheless. If you're betting on don't pass, don't come or making lay bets against the place numbers, you're betting wrong. Playing as a wrong bettor or don't bettor is not as social an experience as betting right—just try finding a table full of wrong bettors rooting against the shooter. If you bet the don't, most of the time you'll be going it alone.

Sometimes right bettors have a problem with that. Some seem to think you've gone over to the Dark Side and are betting against them personally. I've been the recipient of the odd glare or nasty comment when betting on don't pass and don't come. Several years ago, I was signing books at the Empress Casino in Joliet, Illinois, and before the signing had whiled away an hour by making small don't bets. At the signing, a large young fellow, standing 6'4" or so, stopped by my table and bought a book. We chatted for a couple of minutes, and finally he said, "You know what I really can't stand? Wrong bettors. They really, really make me mad."

I was thankful he hadn't been at the craps table with me a little earlier.

13. Place bets: For those who don't want to wait for a come-out roll, or simply want to choose their own point numbers, there are place bets. Large squares on the layout are imprinted with the numbers 4, 5, six, 8, nine and 10. (They appear just that way, with 4, 5, 8 and 10 in numerals and six and nine spelled out. Why? To avoid confusion, because players stand on both sides of the table. A numeral that looks like 6 on one side of the table would look like 9 to players on the other side.)

Place bets are made by putting chips on the layout and asking the dealer for the number. The dealer then will move your chips to that numbered box, in a position that corresponds to your position around the table. That's how the crew keeps track of what bet belongs to what player.

Once you've placed a number, you're rooting for the shooter to roll that number before he rolls a 7. Bet on 5, for instance, and if the shooter rolls a 5 before he rolls a 7, you win. If he rolls a 7 before a 5, you lose.

Are place bets good wagers to make? We'll get into that in "Pass No. 3: Odds and Edges."

14. Buy bets: Buy bets work the same way as place bets. The difference is that on a buy bet, the player pays the house a 5 percent commission in advance, and exchange is paid at true odds when he wins. Essentially, we "buy" a bigger payoff on winning bets. Is it worth our while, and more importantly, worth our cash, to buy instead of place? Check out the next chapter.

15. Hard ways: A shooter rolls a number the hard way when the numbers on both dice are the same. It's 6 the hard way when each die shows a 3.

You can bet on the hard ways to make 4, 6, 8 or 10 by placing chips on the layout and asking the dealer for the hard number. When you do, you're betting that your number will show up the hard way before the shooter rolls either a 7 or your number any other way. For example, if you bet on hard 6, you're betting the shooter will roll a pair of 3s before rolling a 7 or a 6 that shows up either as a 2 and 4 or a 1 and 5.

16. Proposition bets: At the center of the table, there are a whole slew of one-roll wagers available. These are the propositions. You can bet the next roll will be 7. You can bet on 11. You can bet on any craps, which means you'll win if the next roll is 2, 3 or 12, or you can bet 2, 3 or 12 individually. You can bet on "C and E," which is short for "craps and eleven," meaning you win on 2, 3, 11 or 12. You can bet on any of these, but should you? We'll see in the next chapter.

17. Lay bets: These are place bets for wrong bettors. You pay the house a 5 percent commission, then you win if a 7 shows up before the place number. For example, if you lay the 6, you win if the shooter rolls a 7 first, and lose if a 6 turns up before a 7—just the opposite of a place bet on 6.

18. Free odds: One of the few even breaks you'll ever get in the casino is the free odds. After a point is established, pass or come bettors may back up their original bet with a second wager, the free odds. If single odds are offered, then the free odds bet must be the same size as the pass or come bet. Most casinos offer multiple odds, allowing the free odds to be two, three, even 100 times as large as the original bet.

Winning free odds wagers are paid at true odds, meaning there is no house edge on the bet. That makes it to the player's advantage to bet less on pass or come, saving the bulk of the wager for the odds.

Wrong bettors are permitted to lay the odds.

More on free odds in "Pass No. 5: On the Line."

19. Hedge bets: Some players try to cover up the weaknesses in one wager by making another in combination. For example, someone who has a place bet on 6 might also make a smaller bet on any 7, figuring that if he loses the place bet when a 7 turns up, he'll collect on the any 7 wager. He's hedging his bet with the 7. We'll discuss hedges more fully in "Pass No. 9: A Systems Sampler."

20. Field: The field is a one-roll bet that the next roll of the dice will be 2, 3, 4, 9, 10, 11 or 12. The field occupies a very large area on the table layout, and the player can make a field bet simply by placing chips in the field area.

21. Seven out: The shooter sevens out when he rolls a 7 that loses on the pass line. Rolling a 7 on the comeout roll does not seven out because it's a winning roll. Once there's a point number, 7 becomes a losing roll. When the shooter sevens out, his turn as the shooter is over, and the dice pass to the next player.

22. Rails: The craps table is like a large, deep, rectangular box. The layout is at the bottom of the box. On top of the walls, there are grooved inlays just the right size to stand on end the chips you're not currently betting. That groove is the rail. Keep your chips there—you're not permitted to just stack them on the layout where the dice might hit them. One tip: Arrange your chips with higher denominations in the middle and lower denominations on the outside. That way, if a scam artist next to you should try to cop a few chips, he'll be reaching for the lower denominations.

23. Boxman: The boxman is the supervisor at the craps table. Other members of the table crew stand, but the boxman sits at the center of one side of the table. When players buy in, their cash is relayed by the dealers to the boxman, who drops it in a locked box called—strangely enough—a drop box. If any dispute arises at the table, it's the boxman who makes the ruling.

24. Stickman: Another member of the table crew, the stickman, stands on the other side of the table, directly opposite the boxman. He uses a long, curved stick to push the dice to the shooter—hence, "stickman." He's in charge of keeping the game moving, calling out the results of rolls and talking up the game and its bets between rolls. If you walk by a craps table and hear someone calling out, "Dice are hot. Who's on the field? Get those hardways down," that's the stickman. The stickman also is in charge of the center table propositions, instructing the dealers to pay off winning bets and pushing chips from losing wagers over to the boxman.

25. Dealer: While the boxman and stickman stay at the center of opposite sides of the table, two dealers stand farther toward the ends. They handle the roll-to-roll chores of placing bets for players, paying off winners and clearing losing wagers off the layout. When you make place bets, the dealers move your chips into the place number boxes in appropriate positions that they know the bets belong to you. And when you arrive at the table and put cash on the layout, it's the dealer who will give you chips and relay the cash to the boxman.

That's the basic crew—boxman, stickman and two dealers—for a full-size craps table. Any of them will tell you that craps is the hardest game in the casino for table personnel to learn. There are so many bets offered, with different odds and different payouts, that it takes nearly twice as long in dealer's school to learn craps as it does to learn blackjack. Let's move on to those bets and their odds in the next chapter.

Pass No. 3
Odds and Edges

One thing every player must know is that with rare exceptions, the house has an edge on every game in the casino. But where does that house edge come from, and how are the odds calculated? Let's check it out:

1. Rolling two six-sided dice, the possible combinations total:

    A. 12

    B. 24

    C. 36

    D. 48

2. The most frequently occurring roll is:

    A. 6

    B. 7

    C. 8

    D. 11

3. The house gets an edge in craps by:

    A. Limiting the size of bets

    B. Paying at true odds; the odds themselves take care of the edge

    C. Paying at less than true odds

    D. Charging commissions to wrong bettors

4. **The player gets a better deal if the casino pays:**

   A. Odds-for-1
   B. Odds-to-1
   C. Neither; they're the same thing

5. **On the simplest bets, the one-roll propositions, odds are based on:**

   A. The number of ways to roll the proposition number vs. the total number of possible rolls
   B. The number of ways to roll the proposition number vs. the number of ways to roll a 7
   C. Total wagers on all proposition numbers divided by the wagers on any one proposition
   D. The number of players at the table divided by the number of supervisors in the pit

6. **On place bets, odds are based on:**

   A. The number of ways to roll the place number vs. the total number of possible rolls
   B. The number of ways to roll the place number vs. the number of ways to roll a 7
   C. Total wagers on all place numbers divided by the wagers on any one proposition
   D. The number of casinos on the Strip divided by the number of riverboats in Iowa

7. **The most complex wagers for which to calculate the house edge are:**

   A. Field bets
   B. The hard ways
   C. Big Six and Big Eight
   D. Pass, come, don't pass and don't come

8. **Of wagers the player is permitted to make without already having another bet on the table, the lowest house edge is on:**

   A. Pass or come
   B. Don't pass or don't come
   C. Placing the 6 or 8
   D. The field

9. **The wagers with the highest house edges are:**

   A. Big 6 and Big 8
   B. Placing the 4 or 10
   C. The one-roll propositions
   D. The field

10. **When the player makes multiple wagers, the overall house edge is:**

   A. The sum of all the house edges
   B. The highest house edge minus the lowest house edge, provided each bet wins on numbers that cause the others to lose
   C. The average of all the house edges
   D. A weighted average of all the house edges, taking into consideration bet size

Pass No. 3:
Odds and Edges
Answers

1. Rolling two six-sided dice, the possible combinations total:
   C. 36

With six numbers on one die, and six on the other, we just multiply six times six and see there are 36 possible combinations. If we were rolling dodecahedrons, with 12 sides each, instead of six-sided cubes, there would be 12 times 12, or 144 possible combinations, and craps would be a much more confusing game.

2. The most frequently occurring roll is:
   B. 7

There are six combinations of two dice that total 7, compared with one way to make 2, two to make 3, three to make 4, four to make 5, five to make 6, five to make 8, four to make 9, three to make 10, two to make 11 and one to make 12. When I've written this in my newspaper column or explained it at seminars, I've often been asked for an explanation: "What do you mean there are six ways to make 7? You can make it with a 1 and a 6, a 2 and a 5 or a 3 and a 4. That's three ways, not six."

But there are two ways to make each of those combinations. You can make 1 and 6 with the 1 on Die No. 1 and the 6 on Die No. 2, or you can make it with the 1 on Die No. 2 and the 6 on Die No. 1. A good way to visualize it is to use different colored dice—say, one red one and one green one. Then it's easy to see that a 7 made with a red 2 and a green 5 is different than a green 2 and a red 5.

This is important as we consider the relative chances of rolling different numbers. For example, there is only one way to roll a 2—with a 1 on each die. If we don't understand just how many possible two-dice combinations there are, we might be fooled into thinking the odds against rolling a 2 are much smaller than they really are.

3. The house gets an edge in craps by:
> **C.** Paying at less than true odds

In the last answer, we saw that there are 36 possible rolls of the dice, and only one roll that totals 2. That means the true odds against rolling a 2 on any one roll are 35-1—35 ways to make other numbers, one way to make 2.

If the casino paid winning wagers on 2 at 35-1 odds, it would be an even proposition with no house edge. In the long run, the casino would pay out just as much money as it takes in.

That would never do, of course. So instead of 35-1, the casino pays 30-1, and pockets the difference.

4. The player gets a better deal if the casino pays:
> **B.** Odds-to-1

When the casino pays odds-to-1, it gives you your winnings in addition to returning your winning wager. When it pays odds-for-1, the wager is part of the payoff.

For an example, let's go back to the 2 we've been examining in the last two answers. If you make a one-roll bet on 2, the true odds against winning are 35-1. Some casinos pay winning wagers at 30-to-1. Bet $1 and win, and you get back your $1 bet plus $30 in winnings, for a total of $31. Others pay 30-for-1. Bet $1 and win, and you get $30, which includes your original wager.

All this applies mainly to the center-table propositions. You don't have to worry about odds-to-1 vs. odds-for-1 if you're playing the pass/don't pass, come/don't come, the place numbers or the field. And to put it bluntly, the center-table propositions are all lousy bets, as we'll see later. I don't worry much if a craps table is paying odds-for-1; I don't make those bets anyway. But if you like to take a flyer on the propositions, you're better off in a casino that pays odds-to-1.

Winning wagers on pass, come, don't pass and don't come all pay even money. Win a $5 bet, and you'll get $5 in winnings as well as keeping your bet.

We'll discuss all those wagers, as well as the free odds, in "Pass No. 5: On the Line."

5. **On the simplest bets, the one-roll propositions, odds are based on:**

   A. The number of ways to roll the proposition number vs. the total number of possible rolls

We walked through this a little in the last answer. Let's try it with a different number, and say we bet $1 on the one-roll proposition on any 7. There are 36 possible rolls of two dice, and six of them total 7. That means the odds against rolling 7 on any one roll are 30-6, which reduces to 5-1. The casino won't pay you those true odds. You'll get only 4-1 on winning bets.

We'll go over more of the odds, payoffs and house edges for the propositions in "Pass No. 7: The Bad and the Ugly."

6. **On place bets, odds are based on:**

   B. The number of ways to roll the place number vs. the number of ways to roll a 7

On place bets, we are wagering that our number will roll before the next 7. No other numbers matter. So if we make a place bet on 6, what we need to know is that out of 36 possible rolls, there are six ways to make 7 and five ways to make 6. The odds against our winning a place bet on 6 are 6-5. The casino will pay us 7-6, and this is actually one of the better bets on the table.

We'll go over more of the odds, payoffs and house edges for place bets in "Pass No. 6: Place or Buy."

7. **The most complex wagers for which to calculate the house edge are:**

   D. Pass, come, don't pass and don't come

With wagers on pass, come, don't pass and don't come, we're dealing with changing situations and goals. If you've read "Pass No. 2: Definitions," you know that the sequence for a pass bet starts with a comeout roll, on which we win if the roll is 7 or 11, lose if it's 2, 3 or 12 and establish a point number if it's any other roll. If we establish a point number, then 7 becomes a losing roll for us. For pass bettors to win, the shooter must repeat the point before rolling a 7.

To calculate the odds on this wager, we must know the chances of winning with a 7 or 11 on the comeout. We must know the chances of rolling 2, 3 or 12. We must know the chances of establishing each of the six possible point numbers. And we must know the chances of winning or losing with each point number.

I'm not going to run through all that here. The bottom line is that on the pass line, we will win a tiny fraction less than 493 times per 1,000 sequences, making the odds against winning the bet 1.0282-1, the same as on come bets. As for don't pass and don't come, we can say the odds are 1.028-1 if we assume that all bets are played to a decision and that most don't players don't just pick up their bets and leave when they push with a 12 on the comeout. We'll see why we make that distinction in the next answer.

8. Of wagers the player is permitted to make without already having another bet on the table, the lowest house edge is on:
   B. Don't pass or don't come

In the previous question, we figured the odds against winning a pass or come bet at 1.0282-1, while the odds against winning don't pass or don't come are 1.028-1. That translates into a house edge of 1.41 percent on pass or come, and a slightly lower 1.4 percent on don't pass or don't come.

What does that mean? In the long run, the casino wins about $14 of every $1,000 that players wager. That's a narrow enough edge to put these among the best bets in the casino, among those that give the player a fighting chance to walk away a winner, even though the casino will make its share overall.

The house edge on don't pass and don't come is sometimes listed at 1.36 percent instead of 1.4 percent. The lower figure is the house edge if we accept a push as the outcome when the shooter rolls a 2 or a 12 on the comeout. However, if the player simply leaves the wager on the table after a push, betting it on the next sequence starting with a comeout, then that 1.36 percent house edge works against that same wager a second time. The effect of that is to raise the overall house edge on don't pass and don't come to 1.4 percent if we assume all wagers will stay on the table until there is a decision.

9. The wagers with the highest house edges are:

    C. The one-roll-propositions

The field is notoriously bad, with a house edge of 5.6 percent if 2 and 12 both pay 2-1, and 2.7 percent if the 12 pays 3-1. Place bets on 4 or 10 are even worse at 6.67 percent. Big 6 and Big 8 are horrendous at 9.09 percent.

But even Big 6 and Big 8 are better than the best of the one-roll propositions, with house edges that range up to 16.67 percent. Ouch. And double ouch.

Try these on for size: any 7—16.67 percent; any craps—11.1 percent; 2—13.89 percent if the house pays 30-to-1, or 16.67 percent if the payoff is 30-for-1; 12—same as 2; 3—11.1 percent if the house pays 15-to-1, or 16.67 percent if it's 15-for-1.

The hardways aren't one-roll bets, but they're just about as bad. The house has an edge of 9.09 percent if you're betting hard 4 or 10, or 13.89 percent on hard 6 or 8.

As we go along, we'll be comparing the good bets with the bad bets, but here's a big clue: If the proposition is in the center of the layout, between the boxman and the stickman, it's a bet to avoid.

10. When the player makes multiple wagers, the overall house edge is:

    D. A weighted average of all the house edges, taking into consideration bet size

Some players like to make multiple bets, figuring that perhaps the strengths of one wager will cover up the weaknesses in another. It doesn't work quite like that. When we make multiple wagers, we absorb all the strengths and all the weaknesses of each bet.

To demonstrate this without making it unnecessarily confusing, let's take a look at two one-roll bets. Let's say we bet $5 on the field. One of the weaknesses of the field is that the most common roll, 7, is a loser, so we also bet $1 on any 7. Any 7 pays 4-1, so whenever a 7 turns up that costs us $5 on the field, at least we hedge our losses with a $4 win on 7. Right?

Not exactly. We lose more money by adding the bet on 7 than if we just let the field bet stand on its own. Here's how it works.

Let's say we have a perfect sequence of 36 rolls of the dice in which each possible combination shows up once. We bet $5 on the field on each roll, for a total of $180 in field wagers, plus $1 on any 7, for a total of $36 in wagers on 7. Our total risk is $216.

The field pays even money if the roll is 3, 4, 9, 10 or 11, and on the basic version of the bet pays 2-1 if the roll is 2 or 12. Of those 36 rolls, one will be a 12 for a $10 win, one will be a 2 for a $10 win, and we will have $5 wins on two 3s, three 4s, four 9s, three 10s and two 11s. Our total win is $90, and on the 16 winning rolls we also keep our wagers, for another $80. So at the end of the sequence, we have $170 of the $180 we risked on the field. We've lost $10.

On the any 7 bets, we win the six times the shooter rolls a 7. Each time brings us $4 in winnings, worth a total of $24, plus we keep our buck on the six winning rolls, bringing the overall total to $30. We've lost $6 on any 7 in the sequence.

That brings our total losses for the field/any 7 combination to $16 of the $216 we risked. If we divide 16 by 216, we get 0.074, and if we then multiply that by 100 to convert it to a percentage, we see the house edge on the combination is 7.4 percent. That's higher than the 5.6 percent on the field, but lower than 16.67 percent on any 7. It's closer to the house edge on the field, because the field makes up a bigger proportion of our total wager.

Could we have come up with that 7.4 percent figure without going through all the rigamarole of spelling out perfect sequences? Sure. Our wager consists of 5 parts field and 1 part 7, so multiply the 5.6 percent house edge on the field by 5 and add it to one time the 16.67 percent edge on any 7. That gives us 28 plus 16.67, or 44.67. Our total bet is six parts, so we divide 44.67 by 6.

What do you get? 7.4 percent.

OK, most players aren't going to do the arithmetic before they try out a combination, so here's a basic rule. The house edge on a combination will always be higher than the lowest house edge on an individual bet in the combination. (It also will be lower than the highest edge on an individual bet.) Combinations don't cover up weaknesses and lower the overall house edge. They simply add more to house edge in proportion to the sizes of the wagers.

Pass No. 4:
The Match Game

The stickman is responsible for calling out the numbers after each roll. Now, he could simply shout out "Eight!" or "Seven!" before the crew goes about settling bets. But what fun would that be? Instead, stickmen have developed a language of their own with creative terms for each roll. On any of the numbers in the field bet, for example, you might hear, "It's in the field, where the farmers make their money." And you'll hear "Yo-leven!" or just "Yo!" from players and crew alike.

Some calls are individualized—stickmen like to get a little creative with their calls—while some are casino standards. Below you'll find 22 calls—two for each two-dice combination. Match the calls to the numbers.

THE NUMBERS

2.

3.

4.

5.

6.

7.

8.

9.

10.

11.

12.

THE CALLS

A. Puppy paws

B. —— from Decatur

C. Mule teeth

D. ——, no jive

E. Fever

F. Aces

G. Thirty-two juice roll

H. Big Ben, the lady's friend

I. Corner red

J. Big Red

K. Little Joe

L. Yolanda

M. The square pair

N. Australian Yo

O. The lumber number

P. Center field

Q. All the spots we've got

R. Nina from Pasadena

S. Bird Balls

T. Tutu

U. El Diablo

V. The other side of 11's tummy

Pass No. 4:
The Match Game
Answers

2. F and S, aces and bird balls, are both calls for 2, which can be made only with a 1 on each die. Instead of snake eyes, a common enough term even among non-gamblers, you might hear a stickman refer just to the eyes, or say something like, "the ayes have it."

3. N and V, the Australian Yo and the other side of 11's tummy, are descriptive calls for 3. When dice faces totaling 3 are face up, the numbers face down on the table felt total 11—the side opposite the 2 is 5, and the side opposite 1 is 6. So if you see a 1 and a 2, then the 6 and 5, totaling 11, are "Down Under" with their faces on the felt. One common call is acey-deucey, since the only way to make 3 is with a 1 and a 2.

4. K and T, Little Joe and tutu (from two-two), are among the calls for 4. Little Joe is one of many calls that is frequently rhymed, as in "Little Joe from Kokomo," or "Little Joe from Idaho." One of my favorites when the roll is 3-1 is "Baskin-Robbins, 3-1 flavors."

5. E and G, fever and thirty-two juice roll, are nicknames for 5. Some stickmen call it the waitress number. Why? "A pair and a tray [trey]."

6. I and O, corner red and the lumber number, refer to 6. Corner red refers to the big, red number 6 for the Big Six bet placed on a corner of the layout. Many of the calls for 6 have sexual themes. Hang around a craps table for a while, and you'll be sure the number is pronounced "sex."

7. J and U, Big Red and El Diablo, are among the many nicknames for 7. Superstitious players don't like to hear that diabolical number said aloud. Nicknames aside, when the shooter rolls a loser 7, you may hear something like, "Line away, pay the don't," without the nasty number ever being uttered. That indicates to everyone that pass line bets are losers, and the bets on the pass line will be cleared away, while don't bettors will be paid.

8. B and M, —— from Decatur and the square pair, are calls for 8. The full call is "eighter from Decatur"—that would have been a giveaway if I'd put the whole phrase in the questions, wouldn't it? If the 8 consists of two 4s, then the spots are arranged in squares on each die, hence "the square pair." They also can be "windows" or "blocks."

9. P and R, center field and Nina from Pasadena, are calls for 9. Look on the layout for the field bet and you'll see why 9 is center field. Numbers in the field, in order starting from left, are 2, 3, 4, 9, 10, 11 and 12. There are three numbers to the left of 9, three to the right, so the 9 is the center of the field. Change one letter at the end of nine, and you have Nina. Where else would she be from but Pasadena?

10. A and H, puppy paws and Big Ben, the lady's friend, are calls for 10. Puppy paws are for two 5s, just a description of how the spots look. Big Ben is one of many adult-oriented calls for 10 the hard way, along with the zipper ripper or just the ripper.

11. D and L, ——, no jive and Yolanda, are calls for 11. The full phrase is 6-5, no jive, simple rhyming slang that would have been a giveaway in the question. Yolanda is a play off the common call "Yo-leven."

12. C and Q, mule teeth and all the spots we've got, are calls for 12. Like puppy paws for 10, mule teeth is descriptive of the way the spots look on the dice. And what's the maximum number of spots you could see on a roll? If you see 12, that's all the spots we've got.

Pass No. 5
On the Line

Among the best bets in craps are the pass line and don't pass line, along with their close cousins, come and don't come. Both get even better when the backed with free odds.

We looked at the basic rules for pass, don't pass, come and don't come in "Pass No. 2: Definitions," and looked at the house edge in "Pass No. 3: Odds and Edges."

Let's review: A pass line bet starts with a comeout roll. If the comeout is a 7 or 11, pass bettors win. If it's 2, 3 or 12, they lose. Any other number becomes the point, and the shooter must roll that number again before rolling a 7 for pass bettors to win. If a 7 shows up first, pass bettors lose.

Come bets are exactly the same, except they are made when the next roll is not a comeout on the pass line. The next roll serves as a comeout for a pass bet.

Don't pass bets are a slightly distorted mirror image of the pass line. If the comeout roll is a 7 or 11, don't pass bettors lose. If it's a 2 or 3 they win, but if it's 12, they just push and get their money back. Any other number becomes a point. If the shooter rolls a 7 before repeating the point number, don't pass bettors win. If the point number comes first, don't pass bettors lose.

Don't come bets are the same as don't pass, except they're made when the next roll is not a comeout.

Now let's put it all together, along with the free odds:

1. **On the average, a pass, come, don't pass or don't come bet is settled within:**

    A. One roll
    B. Two rolls
    C. Three rolls
    D. Four rolls

2. **Winning wagers on pass, come, don't pass or don't come are paid at:**

    A. Even money
    B. 2-1
    C. Odds that vary with the point number
    D. Even money on the comeout, odds that vary with the point number afterward

3. **For pass bettors, the comeout roll:**

    A. Is the most dangerous roll
    B. Is the most favorable roll
    C. Has the same chance of winning as any other roll

4. **For don't pass bettors, the comeout roll:**

    A. Is the most dangerous roll
    B. Is the most favorable roll
    C. Has the same chance of winning as any other roll

5. **If, after a point is established, the shooter continually rolls numbers that aren't either 7 or the point number:**

    A. The rolls are wasted
    B. He'll probably call for a change of dice
    C. Somebody at the table probably is winning a lot of money

6. **Pass or come bettors may take down their bets:**

    A. Only after a decision has been reached
    B. After a point has been established
    C. If a new player enters the game

7. **Don't pass or don't come bettors may take down their bets:**

   A. Only after a decision has been reached
   B. After a point has been established
   C. If a new player enters the game

8. **If the next roll is not a comeout, a player who wants to make a pass bet:**

   A. May do so, and get the current point number
   B. May do so, and choose a point number
   C. May not do so

9. **If the next roll is not a comeout, a player who wants to make a don't pass bet:**

   A. May do so, and get the current point number
   B. May do so, and choose a point number
   C. May not do so

10. **A player may back a pass or come wager with free odds:**

    A. Only after a point is established
    B. Only before the comeout roll
    C. At any time

11. **A don't pass or don't come player may lay the odds:**

    A. Only after a point is established
    B. Only before the comeout roll
    C. At any time

12. **Free odds wagers pay:**

    A. Even money
    B. 6-5
    C. 3-2
    D. Odds that vary with the point number

13. **The free odds wager:**

    A. Must be the same size as the pass or come bet
    B. Must be twice the size of the pass or come bet
    C. May be of varying sizes, according to house rules

14. On the comeout roll, free odds on come bets usually:

A. Are not at risk

B. Are at risk, the same as at any other time

C. May be doubled

15. For don't pass or don't come bettors, laying the odds pays:

A. Even money

B. 5-6

C. 2-3

D. Odds that vary with the point number

16. The house edge on free odds is:

A. Zero

B. 1.4 percent

C. 10 percent

D. Variable, depending on the point number

17. Backing a pass or come bet by taking free odds, or backing a don't pass or don't come bet by laying the odds:

A. Does not affect the overall house edge

B. Gives the house a slightly bigger edge

C. Reduces the house edge

18. Given the equal-sized bets on the pass line, a player who backs the pass bet with free odds:

A. Will lose more money in the long run than a player who skips the odds

B. Will lose about the same amount of money in the long run as a player who skips the odds

C. Will not only lose less than a player who skips the odds, but will overturn the house edge and win money in the long run

19. Free odds are best used to:

    A. Reduce the initial bet, and reduce exposure to the house edge

    B. Increase the overall bet, giving the player more action on the best bet on the table

    C. Be ignored; skip the odds

20. Don't pass and don't come bettors:

    A. Should skip laying the odds, because they already are the favorites to win after a point is established and laying the odds just waters down their edge

    B. Should reduce the size of their initial bets, then use the difference to lay the odds

    C. Should lay odds in addition to their regular bets

Pass No. 5
On the Line
Answers

1. On the average, a pass, come, don't pass or don't come bet is settled within:

    C. Three rolls

    These bets can be settled in one roll if the comeout is 7, 11, 2, 3 or 12. They can be settled in two rolls if, after establishing a point, the shooter either makes the point or sevens out on the next roll. And the roll can go on indefinitely if, after establishing a point, the shooter keeps rolling anything other than the point or a 7. But the average is about three rolls.

2. Winning wagers on pass, come, don't pass or don't come are paid at:

    A. Even money

    Let's say you bet $10 on the pass line. If the shooter rolls a 7 or 11 on the comeout, you win $10. Let's say that instead, the shooter rolls a 6 on the comeout, then makes his point by rolling another 6. You win $10. The shooter establishes 10 as the point, then makes that. You win $10. No matter what the number is, pass, come, don't pass and don't come pay even money.

3. For pass bettors, the comeout roll:

    B. Is the most favorable roll

    On the comeout roll, pass bettors have eight ways to win—six ways to make a 7 and two ways to make 11. They have four ways to lose—one way to make 12, one way to make 2 and two ways to make 3.

So on the comeout, pass bettors will win twice as often as they lose. The danger is when a point is established. Then, pass bettors become the underdogs. They will lose an average of 6 of every 11 times the point number is 6 or 8; or 3 of every 5 times the point is 5 or 9; or 2 of every 3 times the point is 4 or 10.

It works the same way on come bets. The first roll, serving as a comeout for a come bet, gives the player eight ways to win and only four ways to lose. It's after there's a come point that the player becomes an underdog.

4. For don't pass bettors, the comeout roll:
   A. Is the most dangerous roll

Don't pass is the flip side of the coin from pass. On the comeout, don't pass bettors have only three ways to win—one way to make 2 and two ways to make 3—and eight ways to lose—six ways to make 7 and two ways to make 11.

Once a point is established, though, come bettors are the favorites. Just turn around the numbers from Answer No. 3—don't pass bettors will win an average of 6 of 11 times when the point is 6 or 8; 3 of 5 times when it's 5 or 9; or 2 of 3 times when it's 4 or 10.

Same deal for don't come bettors. The first roll, before a come point has been established, is the most dangerous.

5. If, after a point is established, the shooter continually rolls numbers that aren't either 7 or the point number:
   C. Somebody at the table probably is winning a lot of money

Most players don't simply make one bet and leave it at that. I personally like to make a pass line bet and follow with two come bets until I have three numbers working. Sometimes, if I'm short bankrolled and can't take advantage of free odds (see below), I'll follow a pass bet with place bets on 6 and 8. Others might be betting the hard ways or the center-table propositions so they have action while waiting for their pass or don't pass bets to be settled.

For those who are sticking to pass, come and the place bets, it's good news as long as the shooter rolls numbers that aren't 7. If the point number on the pass line is 9 and I have come bets with points of 4 and 8, then I win any time any of those numbers shows up, and nothing but a 7 can hurt me. The shooter rolls a 12? Fine, can't hurt me, and will win for someone who's betting the field, C and E (next roll must be 2, 3, 11 or 12) or the one-roll proposition on 12. The shooter rolls a 5? Doesn't matter to me. A 3? Doesn't hurt. A 9? Great, I win my come bet on 9, at which point I usually choose to make another come bet.

6. Pass or come bettors may take down their bets:

A. Only after a decision has been reached

It would be pretty cool to be able to take down a pass or come bet after a point has been established, wouldn't it? I'd love to have my bet out there for the comeout, with eight ways to win and only four ways to lose, then be able to take it down when a point has been established and I've become the underdog. Show me a house that lets me do that, and I'll be a 2-1 favorite on every bet. Before long, I'd own the casino, and the first thing I'd do is change the rules so the rest of you wouldn't drive me into bankruptcy.

7. Don't pass or don't come bettors may take down their bets:

B. After a point has been established

Pass bettors can't take their bets down after the comeout roll, but don't pass bettors can. Why? Because after a point has been established, don't pass bettors have passed the danger point and become the favorites. Naturally, the house will let you take down a bet that is likely to cost the casino money.

8. If the next roll is not a comeout, a player who wants to make a pass bet:

A. May do so, and get the current point number

You can do this, but why would you want to? The option is called a put bet, and it'll put you behind the 8 ball. When you make a put bet, you pass up the best part of the pass bet—the comeout roll when you're a 2-1 favorite—and pick up the worst part—after a point has been established and you're the underdog.

Most put bettors will be tempted only if the point number is 6 or 8. That's because other than 7, those are the most frequently rolled numbers. But let's say that with 6 as the point, you make your put bet 11 times, making a $5 wager each time. Your wagers then total $55. There are five ways to roll a winner 6 and six ways to roll a loser 7, so on the average, your 11 bets will bring your five winners. That means you get $25 in winnings and also keep $25 worth of bets on the winners. So at the end of the trial, you have a total of $50 of your original $55. The house winds up with a $5 profit. Divide that $5 by your $55 in wagers, then multiply it by 100 to convert it to a percentage, and you're bucking a house edge of 9.09 percent. That's a big ouch, and that's on the best of the put bets.

If you're in a hurry to get action on the 6 or 8 and don't want to wait for a point to be established on a fresh pass or come bet, then make a place bet on your number (see "Pass No. 6: Place and Buy"). There, you'll be paid $7 for every $6 you wager instead of the even money on the pass line, and the house edge is only 1.52 percent instead of the 9.09 on put bets on 6 or 8.

There is rarely any reason to make a put bet. For an exception, see Answer No. 17 in this section.

9. If the next roll is not a comeout, a player who wants to make a don't pass bet:
   C. May not do so

If the next roll is not a comeout, it means a point has been established. And if a point has been established, don't pass bets are favorites to win. Is the house going to let you make a bet at a point you'd be the mathematical favorite? No way. You can start fresh with a don't come bet, or you can make lay bets (see "Pass No. 6: Place and Buy"). But you can't just bet don't pass on a point that's already established.

10. A player may back a pass or come wager with free odds:

B. Only after a point is established

The free odds are one of the best parts of craps, but you have to wait until a point is established.

11. A don't pass or don't come player may lay the odds:

A. Only after a point is established

Just as with pass and come bettors, don't pass and don't come bettors have to wait before laying the odds. Without a point number, there's nothing on which to base the odds.

12. Free odds wagers pay:

D. Odds that vary with the point number

Free odds are paid at true odds. If the point number is 4, for example, there are three ways to make 4 and six ways to make 7, so the odds against a pass or come bettor winning the wager are 6-3, which reduces to 2-1. Free odds wagers on 4 are paid at 2-1. So are free odds wagers on 10. If the point is 5 or 9, free odds are paid at 3-2, and if the point is 6 or 8, free odds are paid at 6-5.

13. The free odds wager:

C. May be of varying sizes, according to house rules

Traditionally, craps was a single-odds game, meaning the free odds bet had to be the same size as the pass or come bet. Casinos trying to attract more players started to offer double odds, meaning the free odds bet could be twice the size of the original wager. Then came triple odds, and more. Today a few casinos offer 100x odds, in which the free odds wager can be 100 times the pass or come bet. The Stratosphere Tower in Las Vegas even offered 200x odds for a time.

As a practical matter, that's out of reach for most players. With 100x odds, you could back a $5 pass line bet with $500 in odds. That is, you could if you had the bankroll to handle it. But you don't have to take the maximum odds available in order to make the bet. In a casino that offers 100x odds, you can still play single odds, triple odds, 10x odds—whatever makes sense given your bankroll.

And as long as we're on the practical side, let's note that single odds don't always mean a free odds wager of exactly the size of your original bet, nor do triple odds always mean free odds of exactly three times your wager. Casinos will allow you to bet a little more in some instances in order to make the payouts come out even.

Let's say you're wagering $5 on the pass line in a casino that offers single odds, and that the point number is 5. You back your pass bet with $5 in free odds, and the shooter rolls a winner 5. Free odds on 5 pay 3-2, so your winnings on the odds portion of your bet would be $7.50. Making change like that requires time, effort and a lot of change, so the casino streamlines things by allowing you free odds of double the size of your line bet when the point number is 5 or 9. Instead of backing your $5 pass bet with $5 in free odds, you bet $10 in odds instead. Then, if you win, the free odds bet pays $15, and the house can pay you off in $5 chips and not have to keep the small change at the table.

In my neck of the woods near Chicago, riverboat casinos offered single odds when they opened, but after a couple of years several switched to what they touted as "3x, 4x, 5x odds." (Today, 5x odds are common and two local casinos have offered 100x odds.) With 3x, 4x, 5x odds, the casino allows free odds bets of three times your pass line bet if the point is 4 or 10, four times if the point is 5 or 9 and five times if the point is 6 or 8. Why? To make the payoffs easy.

Let's say I'm betting $5 on the pass line, with 3x, 4x, 5x odds. If the point is 4 or 10, I bet $15 in free odds. If I win, my odds are paid at 2-1, and my win is $30. If the point is 5 or 9, I bet $20 in free odds. If I win, I'm paid at 3-2, and I get $30. If the point is 6 or 8, I bet $25 in free odds. If I win, I'm paid at 6-5, and my win is—you guessed it—$30. Nice and even, right?

A friend who was a Las Vegas regular looked at an announcement of 3x, 4x, 5x odds and said, "That's just true triple odds." And it's true, you can get that same deal at casinos that just tout triple odds. Let's say you always backed a pass line bet with exactly three times the amount in free odds, meaning in our example of a $5 line bet, we'd always back it up with $15 in odds. The payoff still comes to a nice, even $30 if the point is 4 or 10, but on 5 or 9 our free odds would win $22.50, and on 6 or 8 we'd win $18. Rather than mess around with quarters, half dollars or $1 tokens, the casino would just as soon let us take a little more odds on some point numbers.

14. On the comeout roll, free odds on come bets usually:
A. Are not at risk

Many craps players don't like to have their free odds working on the comeout roll. If the shooter rolls a 7 on the comeout, it would be a Pyrrhic victory indeed to win a pass line wager while losing much larger free odds bets on come numbers.

Here's how it could happen. Let's say you have a $10 pass bet working with a point number of 9, along with $10 come bets with point numbers of 4 and 6. You also have $40 in odds backing the 9, $30 backing the 4 and $50 backing the 6.

The shooter rolls a 9. Now you win $10 on your pass bet, along with $60 on the free odds backing that 9. Your come bets are still active, but the next roll is a comeout. You put another $10 on the pass line. If the shooter rolls a 7 on the comeout, you win $10 on the pass line, but look how much you stand to lose on the come bets plus odds.

With that in mind, the standard policy in most casinos is that odds on come bets are not working on a comeout unless the player requests it. That way, if you win $10 on the pass line, it's not too much of a disappointment to also lose $20 on the come bets as long as the $80 you have invested in free odds is returned to you.

My own preference is to have the free odds working. The odds don't change. They're still the best bet on the table, even if the next roll is a comeout.

15. For don't pass or don't come bettors, laying the odds pays:
D. Odds that vary with the point number

The odds the casino pays us when we win a free odds bet backing a pass or come bet are the same odds we must lay the casino when backing a don't pass or don't come bet. So if the point number is 6 or 8, a pass bettor who wagers $5 in free odds wins $6, but a don't pass bettor laying the odds must wager $6 to win $5. To put it another way, the pass bettor is paid 6-5 on his free odds, but the don't pass bettor is paid 5-6 when laying the odds.

Similarly, on the other points, laying the odds pays 2-3 on 5 or 9 and 1-2 on 4 or 10.

16. The house edge on free odds is:

A. Zero

There is no house edge on the odds wagers, regardless of whether you're a pass or come bettor taking the free odds, or a don't pass or don't come bettor laying the odds. This is one of the few bets you'll ever see where the casino gives you an even break.

Let's say you're a pass bettor, the point is 5, and you've wagered $10 in free odds. Taking only the odds wager into account, for every 10 times you're in this situation, on average you'll win four times. On each of those four times, you'll be paid 3-2, or $15, and you keep your $10 bet, so you have $25 for each of your four winners. That's a total of $100. How much did you risk? Ten $10 wagers, or $100. Risk equals return. That makes this a dead even bet. The house has no edge.

What if you're laying the odds? Same thing, only in reverse. Now on our average 10 wagers with 5 as the point, we risk $15 each time, for a total risk of $150. Each win pays us $10, plus we keep the $15 bet, so we have $25 for each win. We'll win an average of 6 of 10 times we're on don't pass with a point number of 5. So multiply $25 per win by six wins, and our return is $150. Again, risk equals return.

Whether you're taking the free odds or laying 'em, you're paid at true odds. There is no edge to the house.

17. Backing a pass or come bet by taking free odds, or backing a don't pass or don't come bet by laying the odds:

C. Reduces the house edge

When you start with a pass or come bet, you already have a pretty good bet. The house edge is only 1.41 percent, meaning that on the average, for every $100 you bet, you'll lose $1.41. Don't pass and don't come are slightly better at house edges of 1.4 percent.

Those already are among the better bets in the casino. When you factor in free odds, with no house edge, the overall package dips below 1 percent. If we back our bets with single odds, the overall house edge dips to 0.8 percent, and with double odds the house edge dips a little more, to 0.6 percent. By the time we reach 100x odds, the house edge on the pass-odds combination is down to 0.021 percent—on average, we lose just over 2 cents for every $100 we wager.

That really takes us into the territory of the lowest house edges in the casino. Baccarat, with edges of 1.17 percent on banker and 1.36 percent on player, is good, but not that good. Blackjack has a house edge of about 2 to 2.5 percent against an average player. Those who learn basic strategy can get the house edge down to about 0.5 percent—a little more or a little less, depending on house rules. Given enough free odds, craps players can do even better than basic strategy players.

Who can do better on any casino game? Blackjack card counters and experts on certain video poker games can get an edge on the house. That's about it.

While we're on the subject of reducing the overall house edge, let's go back to the put bet we discussed in Answer No. 8 in this section. On a put bet, the player bets on the pass line after a point has been established. The player misses out on the best part of the pass bet, the comeout roll. It's a lousy deal.

However, a reader of my newspaper column once asked if it might be worth making a put bet on 6 or 8 in order to get the chance to take free odds. Is it possible, he asked, that the overall house edge on the put bet plus odds could be lower than the 1.52 percent on a place bet on 6 or 8?

As it happens, put bets can be useful for bettors who usually make place bets on 6 or 8, provided their bankrolls are big enough. The break-even point is five times odds—a player who puts $5 on the pass line backed with $25 in odds collects $35 on a winner 6. So does a player who makes a $30 place bet on 6. With a lower proportion of free odds in the combination, the place bettor is better off, while with more odds, the put bettor gets more for his money.

18. Given the equal-sized bets on the pass line, a player who backs the pass bet with free odds:
   B. Will lose about the same amount of money in the long run as a player who skips the odds

The 1.41 percent house edge on the pass line (and on come, or the 1.4 percent on don't pass or don't come) remains constant no matter what the size of our free odds wager. By taking free odds, with no house edge, we water down the percentages until it looks as if the house has almost no edge at all, but that edge on our original bet is still there.

Let's do a bit of rounding and say I make 1,000 pass line wagers, betting $1 each time. On the average, I will win 493 times and lose 507, meaning I lose $14.

Now let's say I make 1,000 pass line wagers, betting $1 each time, and each time a point is established I back up my bet with $100 in free odds. I still win 493 times and lose 507, leaving me with $14 in losses on my pass bets. My free odds cancel each other out—on average, I win as much as I lose; that's what a zero house edge means.

Either way, I lose an average of $14. When I'm taking the odds, I'm betting much more money over those thousand rolls. In fact, with the 100x odds in this example, I'm spreading those $14 in losses not over $1,000 in wagers, but over about $667,000 in wagers. Divide $14 in losses by $667,000 in wagers, then convert to percent, and you get a house edge of 0.02 percent that is much lower than the 1.4 percent if you divide $14 in losses by a mere $1,000 in wagers and convert to percent. The house edge on the pass-odds combination is much lower than the house edge on the pass bet alone. But either way, I've lost the same $14, and if I'm taking all those odds I've done it with a lot more risk.

19. Free odds are best used to:
   A. Reduce the initial bet, and reduce exposure to the house edge

Some of you have probably read Answers No. 17 and No. 18 and wondered, "What's the big deal about free odds? The house edge is lower if I take free odds, but my actual average losses are the same as if I didn't. This looks like a numbers game, just a mathematical trick."

So it would be if you always made the same size pass or come bet, regardless of whether you also took the odds. But what if you reduce the size of your pass line bet, shifting part of your overall wager into free odds? Then less of your money is exposed to the 1.41 percent house edge on the pass line, and your long-term expectation improves.

Let's say you're something of a high roller, betting $100 on the pass line. In an average 1,000 sequences in which the pass-line bettor wins 493 times and loses 507, you can expect to lose $1,400 overall.

Now let's say you decide to take single odds. You drop your pass bet to $50, and hold the other $50 in reserve for free odds once a point is established. Over our average 1,000 trials, you break even on the free odds portion of your wager, but your average losses on the pass line now drop to $700. You're getting just as much action, but your average losses are cut in half.

At 20x odds, you cut your pass bet all the way to $5, and gear up to take the big free odds. Again, you have just as much action, and an even better chance to walk away a big winner on a good roll since so much of your wager is being paid at true odds. And your average losses? They drop to only $70 per 1,000 sequences.

That's what makes free odds so valuable. The player who shifts portions of his normal line bet to the odds wager reduces his risk. The more free odds, and the less on the pass line, the better.

If you're less well-bankrolled, it's a different story. If you're at a table with a $5 minimum wager, and you're betting $5 on the pass line, you can't reduce your pass bet when you take odds. You're stuck with that $5 minimum. In an average 1,000 sequences, you'll lose $70 if you take no odds, $70 with single odds, $70 with 20x odds and $70 with a million times odds. Taking the odds does not change your long-term results. But if you're betting any amount above the table minimum, reducing your pass or come bet and shifting the difference into free odds reduces your exposure to the house edge and improves your long-term results.

20. Don't pass and don't come bettors:
    B. Should reduce the size of their initial bets, then use the difference to lay the odds

I've often been asked this one by don't bettors. After a point has been established, don't pass or don't come bettors win more often than they lose. And even though they're the favorites, they're paid at even money. If the point number is 10, for example, don't pass bettors will win an average of two out of every three trials. Not only that, if they've bet $10 and the shooter rolls a 7, they win $10. If they were laying the odds and wanted to win another $10, they'd have risked $20.

Don't pass or don't come bettors are already getting even money on their bets. Why lay the 2-1 odds on 4 or 10, 3-2 on 5 or 9, or 6-5 on 6 or 8? Don't they already have a better deal?

No, they don't. At least they don't when their initial bet is made. On the comeout roll, don't bettors have only three ways to win, and they have eight ways to lose. Lowering the initial wager dramatically reduces the player's exposure on that worst of rolls, the comeout that is the casino's hammer over don't pass and don't come players. Then, players who want more action can take the cash they save through that reduced bet and lay the odds once a point is established.

You reduce exposure to the house edge on the comeout, and shift a portion of your wager into laying the odds, which has no house edge. Good deal.

Pass No. 6:
Place or Buy

Pass, come, don't pass and don't come, coupled with free odds, give bettors the lowest house edge at the craps table. But just which numbers they're rooting for is left to chance—the shooter's roll on the comeout determines that.

Some bettors don't want that chance event to decide their numbers. They want to choose their own. For them, there are place and buy bets.

The basics on how place bets work were described in "Pass No. 2: Definitions." Let's review:

The player can make place bets on any of the six point numbers—4, 5, 6, 8, 9 or 10. Put your bet on the layout, and ask the dealer to place your number for you. If the shooter then rolls your number before the next 7, you win. If the seven comes first, you lose.

Buy bets work exactly the same way, except that the player pays the house a $5 commission along with his bet. In return, the house pays winning buy bets at true odds: If you buy the 4 for $21, the house keeps $1 as its commission, but the remaining $20 is paid at true odds of 2-1 if you win.

Let's see how much you know about place bets and buy bets. While we're at it, we'll check out lay bets—place bets for wrong bettors:

1. **Place bets are paid at:**

    A. 7-6 odds
    B. 7-5 odds
    C. 9-5 odds
    D. Different odds, depending on the place number

2. **The player wins most frequently with place bets on:**

    A. 6 or 8
    B. 5 or 9
    C. 4 or 10

3. **The house edge on place bets:**

    A. Is lowest on 6 or 8
    B. Is lowest on 5 or 9
    C. Is lowest on 4 or 10
    D. Is the same for all place numbers

4. **The player may ask the dealer to take down a place bet:**

    A. Only after at least two rolls
    B. At any time
    C. Only after the bet has been decided

5. **Big 6 and Big 8**

    A. Are the same as place bets on 6 or 8
    B. Are decided the same way as place bets on 6 or 8, but are more costly to the player
    C. Are decided the same way as place bets on 6 or 8, but give the player a better deal

6. **The house makes money on buy bets:**

    A. By charging a commission
    B. By paying less than true odds
    C. By a combination of charging a commission and paying less than true odds

7. **Compared with place bets, the player lowers the house edge by buying:**

    A. 6 or 8
    B. 5 or 9
    C. 4 or 10
    D. Any place number

8. **Lay bets are paid at:**

    A. Even money
    B. 5-6 odds
    C. Odds that depend on the place number

9. **The house makes money on lay bets:**

    A. By charging a commission
    B. By paying less than true odds
    C. By a combination of charging a commission and paying less than true odds

10. **The player faces the lowest house edge when he lays:**

    A. 6 or 8
    B. 5 or 9
    C. 4 or 10
    D. Any number

Pass No. 6: Place or Buy Answers

1. Place bets are paid at:

> **D.** Different odds, depending on the place number

Winning bets pay 7-6 if you're placing 6 or 8, 7-5 if you're placing 5 or 9 or 9-5 if you're placing 4 or 10.

One key point: If you're placing 6 or 8, be sure to bet in multiples of $6. Should you just flip a $5 chip toward the dealer and tell him to place in on 6, you won't get the 7-6 payoff should you win. You'll just be paid even money.

Why? Well, a 7-6 payout on a winning $5 bet in theory would get you winnings of $5.83. The casino isn't about to keep the table stocked with pennies and nickels. You'll get the 7-6 payoff as long as you make your place bets on 6 and 8 in multiples of $6. If you don't, you accept an even-money payoff and a larger house edge.

2. The player wins most frequently with place bets on:

> **A.** 6 or 8

Among the 36 possible combinations on two dice, six add up to 7. So 7, the losing number on place bets, is the number that's rolled most frequently. There are five combinations that total 6 and five that total 8, making those numbers the second most frequently rolled. Then come 5 and 9, with four combinations each, and 4 and 10, with three combinations each.

The bottom line is that the player will win an average of 5 of every 11 place bets on 6 or 8; 4 of every 10 on 5 or 9; and 3 of every 9 on 4 or 10. Another way of expressing that is that the true odds are 6-5 against our winning on 6 or 8; 3-2 on 5 or 9; and 2-1 on 4 or 10. The house has an edge on the bets because the pay-offs listed in Answer No. 1 are less than the true odds.

3.   The house edge on place bets:
   A. Is lowest on 6 or 8

The house edge is 1.52 percent for place bets on 6 or 8, 4 percent on 5 or 9, and 6.67 percent on 4 or 10.

Let's walk through the calculations for the house edge on 5. There are six ways to lose the bet—the six ways to roll the number 7—and four ways to lose—the four ways to roll a 5. On the average, of every 10 times you place a bet on 5, you will win four and lose six.

Say you bet $5 on 5 a total of 10 times, and each possible outcome happens once. You risk a total of $50. On each of the four times you win, you collect $7 in winnings, plus keep your $5 wager, for a total of $12 each time. So at the end of our 10-bet sequence, you have $48 left. That means the house has kept $2 of your original $50. Divide the $2 in losses by the $50 in risk, and you get 0.04. Multiply by 100 to convert to percent, and you find that the house edge is 4 percent.

When comparing house edges on the place bets, we find two very attractive numbers, and four not worth worrying about. The 1.52 percent house edge on 6 or 8 isn't quite as good as the 1.41 percent on pass or come, or the 1.4 percent on don't pass or don't come, and it doesn't afford us the opportunity to take free odds. Still, it's one of the lower house edges in the casino, and place bets on 6 or 8 will give us a good run for our money.

Place bets on the other numbers are a different matter. That 4 percent house edge on 5 or 9 is nearly triple the house edge on the pass line, and the 6.67 percent house edge on 4 or 10 is nearly 5 times the edge on pass. Why would we make these bets? There's no reason at all, unless we're so desperate for action that we don't mind throwing our money away.

When I give seminars for craps beginners, I walk them through pass and come, then through don't pass and don't come, then the free odds, and finally through place bets on 6 and 8. Then I tell them that if they stick to those bets and never learn another thing about craps, they'll give themselves a better shot at winning than the sharpies who are throwing money at place numbers across the board, or on the hardways or on any of the one-roll bets we'll discuss in the next chapter.

Pass, come, don't pass, don't come, place bets on 6 and 8—these are essentials of craps. The other bets on the table are essential mainly to the house. They help pay for the chandeliers.

4. The player may ask the dealer to take down a place bet:
   B. At any time

Unlike pass line bets, which we must leave in play until a decision has been reached, place bets may be taken down at any time. The key difference is that on the comeout roll, a pass bettor is the favorite to win, but the house becomes the favorite after a point is established. If our bet is on the table when we're the favorite, the house certainly isn't going to let us take it down when we become the underdog.

Place bets are different. We're never the favorite on a place bet. The house edge is unchanging, the same on every roll. Under those circumstances, the house will allow us to take the bet down if we want to walk away or just feel luckier with another wager.

5. Big 6 and Big 8:
   B. Are decided the same way as place bets on 6 or 8, but are more costly to the player

At the corner of the layout, near the field bet, you can see boxes with a big "6" and a big "8." If you tell the dealer you want to bet on Big 6 or Big 8, that's where your money goes.

The bets work just like place bets. Bet Big 6, and if the shooter rolls a 6 before the next 7, you win, and if the 7 comes first, you lose.

One problem. Big 6 and Big 8 pay just even money, not the 7-6 odds if you place 6 or 8 instead. Without those odds, the house edge soars to 9.09 percent. There is no reason ever to bet Big 6 or Big 8. If you want those numbers, place 6 or 8 instead.

6. The house makes money on buy bets:
   A. By charging a commission

This one's a gimme, just to see who's paying attention. The commission on buy bets, and how it works, was described in the introduction to this chapter.

Once you've paid the commission, buy bets pay at true odds. So if you buy 6 or 8, instead of a 7-6 payoff, you'll get 6-5; on 5 or 9, instead of 7-5 you'll get 3-2; and on 4 or 10, instead of 9-5, you'll get 2-1.

Sound good? Not so fast. Move on to the next answer.

7. Compared with place bets, the player lowers the house edge by buying:
   C. 4 or 10

On buy bets, you pay a 5 percent commission in exchange for getting true odds on the place numbers. Problem: The house edge on place bets on 6, 8, 5 and 9 is lower than that 5 percent you're paying in commission. Buying those numbers is a waste of your time and money. You're better off with the place bets.

The exceptions are 4 and 10. On those numbers, the house edge is 6.67 percent, so paying the commission in order to get true odds lowers the overall house edge to 4.76 percent. That's still not a great deal as craps bets go, but it's a much better deal than you get by placing 4 or 10 instead.

My friend and fellow Bonus Books author, Frank Scoblete, has another take on buy bets, which he describes in his book *Forever Craps*. What if you find a casino willing to stretch the bet size for which it takes a $1 commission? If you offer to buy the 5 for $30, a 5 percent commission would be $1.50. Maybe the casino doesn't want to deal with the change, and will charge you only a $1 commission. With a bigger bet paid at true odds, while the commission remains at $1, the house edge drops.

Frank says he's pushed it to buying the 5 or 9 for $38, which with a $1 commission yields a house edge of 2.56 percent.

Not every house will permit a move like that, but serious place/buy bettors may want to check it out both at the tables and in *Forever Craps*.

8. Lay bets are paid at:
C. Odds that depend on the place number

Lay bets are place/buy bets for wrong bettors. If you lay the 6, you're not betting the shooter will make a 6 before the 7, you're betting the shooter will roll a 7 before the 6.

When you make the lay bet, you pay the house a commission based on 5 percent of your potential payoff. When you win, you are paid at true odds—5-6 when you lay the 6 or 8, 2-3 when you lay the 5 or 9, or 1-2 when you lay the 4 or 10.

Let's say you lay the 6 for $24. At 5-6 odds, if the shooter rolls a 7, you win $20. So when you make the bet, you pay the house a $1 commission, representing 5 percent of your potential $20 win.

9. The house makes money on lay bets:
A. By charging a commission

Lay bets are paid off at true odds, so there is no house edge other than the commission. If you made lay bets from here to eternity, and the house did not charge a commission, you would break even.

10. The player faces the lowest house edge when he lays:
C. 4 or 10

For lay bettors, 6 and 8 are not the players' friends as they are for place bettors. In fact the house edge is highest, at 4 percent, on lay bets on 6 and 8. It's a little lower, at 3.23 percent, on 5 or 9 and at its lowest, 2.44 percent, on 4 or 10.

Let's walk through the arithmetic on a lay bet. Let's say you're laying the 10 for $40. You're paid at 1-2 odds, making your potential win $20. Five percent of $20 is $1, so you pay the house a $1 commission per wager. That makes your total risk $41 per bet.

There are six combinations of two dice that total 7 and only three that total 10, so on the average you will win a lay bet on 10 six times for every three times you lose. In an average nine bets, you risk 9 times $41, or $369. Each time you win, you get $20 in winnings plus keep your $40 wager, for a total return to you of $60 per win. Multiply that $60 times 6 wins, and at the end of our nine wagers you are left with $360 of your original $369. The house keeps $9. Divide that $9 loss by $369 in wagers, and you get 0.0244. Multiply that number by 100 to convert it to a percentage, and the house edge is 2.44 percent.

That's close enough to double the 1.4 percent house edge on don't pass and don't come that I shy away from laying the place numbers. I'd rather stick with don't pass, don't come and laying the odds.

Pass No. 7:
The Bad and the Ugly

In the last two chapters, we've focused on the best bets in craps. Pass or don't pass, come or don't come, free odds, place bets on 6 or 8—those are the bets that give the lowest edge to the house.

Now let's look at the bets that give a little something extra— to the house. Whether you're betting the hardways or any of the one-roll propositions, you're giving the casino a big advantage.

Before we move into this set of questions and answers, let's list bets and payoffs for wagers in this section:

Field: Even money if the roll is 3, 4, 9, 10 or 11, or 2-1 if the roll is 2 or 12. (Some casinos pay 3-1 on 12.)

2: 30-1 or 30-for-1

3: 15-1 or 15-for-1

11: 15-1 or 15-for-1

12: 30-1 or 30-for-1

Any 7: 4-1

Any craps: 7-1

Hardway 4: 7-1

Hardway 6: 9-1

Hardway 8: 9-1

Hardway: 7-1

**C and E,
or Craps and Eleven**: 4-1

The center-table propositions can be tempting, in part because minimum bets are usually low. A table with $5 or $10 minimum bets on the pass line might take $1 bets on the propositions. Some low-minimum tables in downtown Las Vegas will even permit 25-cent proposition wagers. And some players are willing to give the house its big edge in hopes of making a quick, big hit. After all, pass line bets pay only even money, placing 6 or 8 pays only 7-6 odds, but a one-roll proposition on 12 pays 30-1, and winning an even-money bet can't match the thrill of hitting a 30-1 shot.

But that's jackpot thinking, low-percentage thinking. It's taking the appeal of slot machines and applying it to a table games setting. Is that appeal worth it in a game that offers much better percentage bets? I don't think so, but let's see what you think.

1. On the any craps bet, the player wins if the shooter rolls:

    A. 2 or 3
    B. 2 or 12
    C. 2, 3 or 12

2. On C and E, the player wins if the shooter rolls:

    A. 2, 3 or 11
    B. 2, 11 or 12
    C. 2, 3, 11 or 12

3. A player who bets the center-table proposition on 2 wins if:

    A. A 2 is rolled before the next 7
    B. The next roll is a 2
    C. Either one of the dice shows a 2

4. Players who bet on the one-roll proposition on 12 are better off if:

    A. The payoff is 30-to-1
    B. The payoff is 30-for-1
    C. Either; they are the same thing

5. **The horn:**

>   A. Is a bet that pays on the same numbers as C and E
>   B. Is a bet that pays on craps or 7
>   C. Is sounded when it's time for a new crew to start its shift

6. **Three-way craps:**

>   A. Is a variation in which a shooter who rolls three craps in a row wins a progressive jackpot
>   B. Is played at a small table with only three players and one dealer
>   C. Is a bet that pays on the same numbers as any craps

7. **If the casino pays odds-for-1, the highest house edge among one-roll bets is a tie among:**

>   A. 2 and 12
>   B. 3 and 11
>   C. Any 7, 2, 3, 11, 12 and C and E, the horn and 3-way craps

8. **If the house pays odds-to-1, the highest house edge among one-roll bets is on:**

>   A. 3 or 11
>   B. 2 or 12
>   C. Any 7 or C and E

9. **A hop bet is:**

>   A. A bet not marked on the layout that permits the player to bet on any specific combination of the two dice
>   B. A one- or two-roll bet that allows the player's bet to "hop" to the second roll if the wagered number does not hit on the first
>   C. A bet that one die will hop off the table

10. Wrong bettors may take the opposite side of one-roll propositions by:

    A. Paying the house a commission

    B. Laying bigger odds than the true odds of the bet

    C. Never; the house does not book one-roll lay bets

11. The common one-roll bet that gives players the most chances to win is:

    A. The field

    B. C and E

    C. Any 7

12. A casino that wants to lower the house edge on the field bet usually:

    A. Adds another number to the field

    B. Declares the bet a push if the shooter rolls a 7 as a 1 and a 6

    C. Pays extra on 12

13. Hardway bets are settled in:

    A. One roll

    B. Two rolls

    C. One or more rolls; it depends on the rolls

14. Hardway bets are available for:

    A. Any even point number

    B. Any point number

    C. Any number

15. The house edge is lowest on:

    A. Hard 6 or 8

    B. Hard 4 or 10

    C. Any; the house edge is always the same on the hardways

Pass No. 7:
The Bad and the Ugly
Answers

1. On the any craps bet, the player wins if the shooter rolls:

    C. 2, 3 or 12

Those numbers—2, 3 or 12—are the ones that are called craps. Any craps is a one-roll bet. If the shooter rolls 2, 3 or 12, the bettor wins. If the roll is any other number, the bettor loses.

2. On C and E, the player wins if the shooter rolls:

    C. 2, 3, 11 or 12

C and E stands for craps and eleven, so the player wins if the roll is craps—2, 3, or 12—or 11.

3. A player who bets the center-table proposition on 2 wins if:

    B. The next roll is a 2

Except for the hardways, the bets you'll find at the center of the table are less involved than the pass line or the place bets. There's no waiting for a 7. If your number doesn't come up on the first roll, you lose. The instant action of these bets, with decisions on every roll, is part of the attraction. Unfortunately, the house edges are so high the one-roll propositions are really just chip-eaters.

4. Players who bet on the one-roll proposition on 12 are better off if:

   A. The payoff is 30-to-1

Here's a little review for those who skipped "Pass No. 2: Definitions." The difference is that in odds-for-1, your bet is considered part of your overall return, but in odds-to-1, you receive your winnings and you have your bet returned to you. So if you bet $1 on 12 and win, 30-for-1 odds bring you a total return of $30, while 30-to-1 odds bring you $30 in winnings plus a return of your $1 bet, for a total of $31.

The only place at the gaming tables you're likely to see odds-for-1 payoffs are on certain one-roll propositions in craps. Bets on 12 will pay 30-1 at some casinos, and 30-for-1 at others. So will bets on 2. Bets on 11 and on 3 will pay 15-to-1 at some casinos, and 15-for-1 at others. Some casinos pay hop bets (see below) at odds-to-1, others at odds-for-1.

How do you find out the payoffs at your favorite casino? Just look at the table layout. Toward the center of the table, boxes will be lined off for the propositions. The box for one-roll wagers on 12, for instance, will have a picture of two dice, each showing six spots. Underneath will be the payoffs on the bets. If it says 30-for-1, you're getting the worst of the deal.

Even at casinos that pay odds-for-1 on some propositions, most wagers pay odds-to-1. When you make the place wager on 6 described in the last chapter, you're paid 7-to-6, a pretty good deal with a house edge of 1.52 percent, not 7-for-6, which would be a horrendous deal with a house edge of 46.97 percent.

Better I should have a long-running account with my friendly neighborhood loan shark than to make a bet like that.

The hardways pay at odds-to-1 just about everywhere. So do one-roll propositions on any 7 or any craps. Since odds-to-1 is by far the more common method, you'll usually just see 30-1 when a gambling analyst or author means 30-to-1, but the less common 30-for-1 will be spelled out.

By the way, there is one other casino game in which the common payoff is for-1 instead of to-1. That's video poker.

5. The horn:

A. Is a bet that pays on the same numbers as C and E

Both the horn and C and E pay on 2, 3, 11 or 12, but the horn does it by breaking down your wager into four separate bets. If you bet $4 on the horn, the dealer will break it down into $1 bets on 2, 3, 11 and 12. And instead of the overall 4-1 payoff you get on C and E, the horn pays as four separate bets. Any time you win, you'll also lose the other three parts of your wager, but you'll get either 30-1 or 30-for-1 on the winning portion of your bet if the roll is 2 or 12 and 15-1 or 15-for-1 if the roll is 3 or 11.

Let's say we're in a casino that pays odds-to-1, and we bet $4 on the horn in a perfect sequence of 36 rolls in which each possible combination comes up once. We risk a total of $144. The one time the roll is a 2, we get back $31—$30 in winnings plus the $1 of our wager that was on 2. We also get $31 on the one 12, and we get $16 on each of the two 3s and two 11s. Add all that up, and at the end of the sequence we have $126. Our total losses are $18. Divide the $18 by the $144 we risked, then multiply it by 100 to convert it to a percentage, and we get a house edge of 12.5 percent. That makes the horn a little better bet than C and E, which has a house edge of 16.67 percent.

However, if we're in a casino that pays odds-for-1, our overall return is $1 less on each of our six winning rolls, and our average losses rise to $24 for our $144 in wagers. That's a house edge of 16.67 percent—the same as C and E.

Horn bets must be made in multiples of $4, so the wagers can be evenly divided among the four winning numbers.

There are three horn variations which must be made in multiples of $5. One is the horn high, in which a $5 bet gives the player $1 bets on 2, 3 and 11, and a $2 bet on 12. The horn low puts the $2 bet on 2, with $1 each on 3, 11 and 12. And then there's the horn high yo, which puts the $2 bet on 11.

If the house pays odds-to-1, the house edge rises slightly to 12.8 percent on horn high and horn low, while decreasing slightly to 12.2 percent on horn high yo. If payoffs are odds-for-1, the house edge remains steady at (aaarrgggghhh!) 16.67 percent.

6. Three-way craps:

    C. Is a bet that pays on the same numbers as any craps

The 3-way craps bet works the same way as the horn, except without the 11. A $3 bet is broken down into three $1 bets, with $1 on 2, $1 on 3 and $1 on 12. As in the horn, each portion of the bet is decided separately, with a 30-1 or 30-for-1 payoff on 2 or 12 and 15-1 or 15-for-1 on 3. The house edge is 12.97 percent if the casino pays odds-to-1, and 16.67 percent if it pays odds-for-1.

The player is better off with any craps, which pays 7-1 regardless of whether the roll is 2, 3 or 12, and the house edge is 11.1 percent.

7. If the casino pays odds-for-1, the highest house edge among one-roll bets is a tie among:

    C. Any 7, 2, 3, 11, 12, C and E, the horn and 3-way craps

On all those bets, the house edge is 16.67 percent—on average, for every $100 you wager, you'll lose $16.67. Compare that with the 1.41 percent house edge on the pass line or the 1.52 percent on placing 6 or 8, and you'll understand why I caution players to stay away from the center table propositions.

Let's walk through calculating the house edge on 2 if the payoff is 30-for-1. Of 36 possible rolls of two dice, only one totals 2—a 1 on each die. If I bet $1 on 2 in a perfect sequence of 36 rolls in which each possible combination shoes up once, I will risk a total of $36. The one time I win, my return is $30, leaving me with a net loss of $6. Divide the $6 in losses by my $36 risk, and you get 0.1667. Multiply that number by 100 to convert it to a percentage, and the house edge is 16.67 percent. Yuck.

8. If the house pays odds-to-1, the highest house edge among one-roll bets is on:

    C. Any 7 or C and E

Experienced craps players have often told me they were surprised that the edge on any 7 is that high. It's a favorite among many players to use as a hedge, to protect their pass line bets against a loser 7. The problem is that there are six ways to roll a 7, and 30 ways to roll anything else. That makes the true odds against rolling a 7 on any one roll 5-1. But the bet pays only 4-1—that's 4-to-1, even if some other one-roll propositions pay odds-for-1. That's enough of a shortfall that the house edge is a whopping 16.67 percent.

C and E, or craps and eleven, works out the same way. The C and E bettor wins if the shooter rolls craps, which is 2, 3 or 12, or 11. There is one way to roll 2, one way to roll 12, two ways to roll 3 and two ways to roll 11. That makes six ways to roll a winning number on this bet out of the 36 possible combinations on two dice. True odds are 30-6, which reduces to 5-1. You're paid only 4-1, and in the long run, you'll lose $16.67 for every $100 you wager.

9. A hop bet is:
A. A bet not marked on the layout that permits the player to bet on any specific combination of the two dice

Players can ask the dealer for 3-3 on the hop, or 2-4 on the hop, or any other specific combination. If both numbers are the same in your combination, the house will pay 30-1 (house edge 13.89 percent) or 30-for-1 (house edge 16.67 percent). If the numbers are different, the house will pay 15-1 (house edge 11.1 percent) or 15-for-1 (house edge 16.67 percent).

10. Wrong bettors may take the opposite side of one-roll propositions by:
B. Laying bigger odds than the true odds of the bet

This is not commonly done. There are plenty of players willing to risk a buck for the chance of a $30 payoff if the next roll is 12. It's a cheap thrill. "What's a buck?" they figure, and plunge into the deep end of the house edge pool. On the other hand, laying the one-roll numbers is no cheap thrill. To lay the 12, you'll have to risk $37, and if you win, you collect only $1. This time, those who ask, "What's a buck?" shy way from small rewards for a big risk. Good for them. If you're going to bet against the shooter, stick to don't pass and don't come.

11. The common one-roll bet that gives players the most chances to win is:

A. The field

Field bets win if the roll is 2, 3, 4, 9, 10, 11 or 12. There's one way to roll 2, two ways to roll 3, three ways to roll 4, four ways to roll 9, three ways to roll 10, two ways to roll 11 and one way to roll 12. That's a total of 16 possible winning rolls out of the 36 two-dice combinations.

All those winning numbers make the field a very attractive bet for beginners. It's easy because it's decided in one roll. There's no waiting around for point numbers or seeing if a 7 rolls first. The field has a great, big area on the layout in which players can place their own bets. Inexperienced players flock to it. But while the house edge is lower than that on other one-roll bets, the field still gives the casino too big an advantage to place it on the good side of the wager ledger. We'll look at that in the next answer.

12. A casino that wants to lower the house edge on the field bet usually:

C. Pays extra on 12

The standard field bet pays even money if the roll is 3, 4, 9, 10 or 11, but pays 2-1 if the roll is 2 or 12. Some casinos pay 3-1 on 12, cutting the overall house edge.

Let's take a look at the house edge. If I bet $1 on the field on each of 36 rolls in which each combination comes up once, I risk $36. On each of my 16 winning bets, I get my dollar wager back. I also get $1 in winnings on each of my 14 winners on 3, 4, 9, 10 and 11, and I get $2 on my one 2 and $2 on my one 12. So at the end of the sequence, I have $34 left of my original $36. Divide my $2 in losses by the $36 risk, and multiply it by 100 to convert it to a percentage, and the house edge is 5.56 percent.

When the house raises the payoff on 12 to 3-1, my losses drop to $1 per $36 wagered, and the house edge falls to 2.78 percent.

I once even encountered a field bet that paid 3-1 on both 2

and 12. That entirely eliminates the house edge—it's an even bet. Harrah's in Joliet, Illinois, offered that wager for a while. They were counting on the bet attracting players who would also make other bets while they were there. I spent a pleasant couple of hours there, making field bets and avoiding anything that had a house edge of any size. I had a few Diet Cokes on the house (Illinois casinos are not permitted to serve complimentary alcoholic beverages), got lucky on a few 2s and 12s and walked away with a nice profit. Had normal payoffs been in effect, I'd have lost a little money . . . well, to be honest, with normal payoffs I wouldn't have been betting the field.

In either the version with the 5.56 percent house edge or the one with the 2.78 percent house edge, the field is better than other one-roll bets, but still much worse than the pass line or placing 6 or 8. Not only is the house edge lower on pass at 1.41 percent or placing 6 or 8 at 1.52 percent, but it takes more than one roll to decide those bets. The house edge on the field when 12 pays 2-1 is about 4 times the house edge on pass, and the bet is settled nearly three times as fast.

You lose your money more than 10 times as fast on the field as on the pass line. Looking for a silver lining? At least the field isn't as bad as any 7. On any 7, you lose your money three times as fast as on the field.

13. Hardway bets are settled in:
   C. One or more rolls; it depends on the rolls.

On the hardways, you're betting that your number will be rolled with both dice showing the same number before either a 7 or your number rolled any other way comes up. For example, on a hard 6, you're betting that the shooter will roll a pair of 3s before rolling either 1-5, 2-4 or any total of 7.

The bet can stay on the table for several rolls if the shooter is rolling other numbers. Say you bet on hard 6, and the shooter rolls 5, 9, 11, 3, 12 . . . none of those rolls affect your bet, so it stays on the table until the shooter rolls either a 6 or a 7. On the other hand, the shooter could roll a 6 or a 7 right after you place your bet. Then the wager is settled in one roll.

14. Hardway bets are available for:

    A. Any even point number

Hardway bets are available on 4, 6, 8 or 10. There are no hardway bets on odd numbers because there is no way to roll an odd total with both dice showing the same number—any number added to itself yields an even number. And there are no hardway bets on the even numbers 2 and 12 because they can be rolled ONLY with both dice showing the same number.

15. The house edge is lowest on:

    A. Hard 6 or 8

There are five ways to roll 6, only one of which is the hard way—3 on each die. That leaves four losing ways to roll 6. Along with the six ways to roll a loser 7, the true odds on winning a hardway bet on 6 are 10-1. The house pays only 9-1, and the house edge is 9.09 percent. The arithmetic is the same on hard 8.

On hard 4 or hard 10, the true odds are 8-1, but the house pays only 7-1, and the house edge is 11.1 percent.

Pass No. 8:
Getting Edgy

In the last few chapters, we've mentioned house edges on many bets. Let's bring them all together now and put it in context.

For each of the 20 wagers listed below, decide whether the house edge is low (less than 2 percent, medium (2 percent) to 7 percent) or high (more than 7 percent):

1. **Field**

   A. Low
   B. Medium
   C. High

2. **Hard 6 or 8**

   A. Low
   B. Medium
   C. High

3. **Don't pass or don't come**

   A. Low
   B. Medium
   C. High

4. **One-roll 12**

   A. Low
   B. Medium
   C. High

5. Horn

    A. Low

    B. Medium

    C. High

6. Place 4 or 10

    A. Low

    B. Medium

    C. High

7. Pass or come

    A. Low

    B. Medium

    C. High

8. Lay 6 or 8

    A. Low

    B. Medium

    C. High

9. Big 6 or Big 8

    A. Low

    B. Medium

    C. High

10. Lay 5 or 9

    A. Low

    B. Medium

    C. High

11. Place 6 or 8

    A. Low

    B. Medium

    C. High

12. C and E

    A. Low

    B. Medium

    C. High

13. One-roll 11

    A. Low

    B. Medium

    C. High

14. Free odds

    A. Low

    B. Medium

    C. High

15. Lay 4 or 10

    A. Low

    B. Medium

    C. High

16. Any craps

    A. Low

    B. Medium

    C. High

17. Place 5 or 9

    A. Low

    B. Medium

    C. High

18. Hop bet

    A. Low

    B. Medium

    C. High

19. Any 7

    A. Low
    B. Medium
    C. High

20. Buy 4 or 10

    A. Low
    B. Medium
    C. High

Pass No. 8: Getting Edgy Answers

Let's just let the numbers speak for themselves in this set of answers. More details on all of these bets can be found in the previous three chapters.

For the record, the bets with low house edges of less than 2 percent are No. 3, don't pass or don't come; No. 7, pass or come; No. 11, place 6 and place 8; and No. 14, the free odds.

1. **Field:**
   B. Medium (5.56 percent if 12 pays 2-1; 2.78 percent if 12 pays 3-1)

2. **Hard 6 or 8:**
   C. High (9.09 percent)

3. **Don't pass or don't come:**
   A. Low (1.4 percent)

4. **One-roll 12:**
   C. High (13.89 percent if it pays 30-1; 16.67 percent if 30-for-1)

5. **Horn:**
   C. High (12.5 percent if the house pays odds-to-1; 16.67 percent if it pays odds-for-1)

6. Place 4 or 10:
>   **B.** Medium (6.67 percent)

7. Pass or come:
>   **A.** Low (1.41 percent)

8. Lay 6 or 8:
>   **B.** Medium (4 percent)

9. Big 6 or Big 8:
>   **C.** High (9.09 percent)

10. Lay 5 or 9:
>   **B.** Medium (3.23 percent)

11. Place 6 or 8:
>   **A.** Low (1.52 percent)

12. C and E:
>   **C.** High (16.67 percent)

13. One-roll 11:
>   **C.** High (11.1 percent if the house pays 15-1; 16.67 percent if 15-for-1)

14. Free odds:
>   **A.** Low (Zero; there is no house edge on either taking the odds to back pass or come bets or laying the odds to back don't pass or don't come bets)

15. Lay 4 or 10:
>   **B.** Medium (2.44 percent)

16. Any craps:
>   **C.** High (11.1 percent)

17. Place 5 or 9:

    B. Medium (4 percent)

18. Hop bet:

    C. High (If both dice are to land on the same number, such as 3-3 on the hop, 13.89 percent if the house pays 30-1 and 16.67 percent if 30-for-1; if the numbers are different, such as 2-4 on the hop, 11.1 percent if the house pays 15-1 and 16.67 percent if 15-for-1.)

19. Any 7:

    C. High (16.67 percent)

20. Buy 4 or 10:

    B. Medium (4.76 percent)

Pass No. 9:
A Systems Sampler

Few craps players are happy to have just one bet on the table. Whether they're looking for lots of action or seeking that perfectly balanced combination of bets that will beat the house, players like to have lots of numbers working.

Let's explore some systems, along with their strengths and weaknesses:

1. **A player who wants to have action on three or more numbers gets the lowest house edge by:**

    A. Combining a pass line bet with place bets on 6 and 8
    B. Placing 6 and 8 and buying either 4 or 10
    C. Betting either pass or don't pass, followed by two come or don't come bets until three numbers are working, and backing all bets with free odds

2. **A short-bankrolled player who wants three numbers working but can't afford take free odds faces the lowest house edge by:**

    A. Combining a pass line bet with place bets on 6 and 8
    B. Placing 6 and 8 and buying either 4 or 10
    C. Making a pass or don't pass bet, followed by two come or don't come bets, even without the free odds

3. **Opening with a pass bet, then placing 6 and 8 (or only one of them, if the other is the point):**

   A. Doubles the player's average expected loss compared to sticking with pass and come
   B. Gives the player the two point numbers most likely to win
   C. Gives the player a long-term edge over the house

4. **Waiting to bet until the shooter makes a pass or two, or at least rolls a few numbers without rolling a 7:**

   A. Ensures the player is betting at a hot table
   B. Reduces the player's exposure to the house edge
   C. Increases the house edge, because the player has missed out on point numbers already rolled

5. **A pass-line bettor who hedges by betting on any craps on the comeout roll:**

   A. Gives little extra edge to the house
   B. Decreases the house edge by winning the any craps bet on rolls that are losers on the pass line
   C. Has results no different in the long run than betting the pass line alone

6. **A pass-line bettor who hedges by betting on any 7 after a point has been established:**

   A. Gives little extra edge to the house
   B. Decreases the house edge by winning the any 7 bet on rolls that are losers on the pass line
   C. Has results no different in the long run than betting the pass line alone

7. **Betting $26 across or $27 across gives the player:**

   A. $1 bets on each of the one-roll propositions plus the hardways
   B. Covers all possible rolls by spreading bets across any 7, any craps and all the place numbers
   C. Bets on every place number except the point on the pass line

8. **Darby's Field, also known as the dinner bet:**

    A. Is a sure-fire way to win enough money for dinner
    B. Will win more often than it loses
    C. Is the one combination of bets that gives the player a mathematical edge over the house

9. **Combination bets give the player:**

    A. A way to cover up the weaknesses in a bet
    B. A way to gain an edge over the house
    C. All the strengths and all the weaknesses in each bet in the combination

10. **Money management systems:**

    A. Can make the player a winner in the long run
    B. Can help the player extend play
    C. Are an important component of the house edge and must be included in any meaningful calculations

Pass No. 9:
A Systems Sampler
Answers

1. **A player who wants to have action on three or more numbers gets the lowest house edge by:**

    C. Betting either pass or don't pass, followed by two come or don't come bets until three numbers are working, and backing all bets with free odds

    Whenever I'm playing with sufficient bankroll to take advantage of the free odds, that's my favored method. As we've seen, the house edge is only 1.41 percent on pass or come, and only 1.4 percent on don't pass or don't come. Back your bets with single odds, and you lower the overall house edge to 0.8 percent. That drops to 0.6 percent with double odds, 0.5 percent with triple odds, 0.3 percent with 5x odds and 0.2 percent with 10x odds.

    Here's the way it works. I start with a bet on the pass line. If the comeout roll is a point number, I back it with odds and make a come bet. If the next roll is a different point number, I back the come bet with odds, then make a second come bet. Then, if the shooter rolls another point number, I back the second come bet and wait for the outcome.

    Let's say I'm playing at a table with $5 minimum bets that offers the 3x, 4x, 5x odds that are common in my home area near Chicago. (For a full description, see "Pass No. 5: On the Line.") I bet $5 on the pass line, and the roll is 5. I back the 5 with $20 in free odds, and make a $5 come bet. If the next roll is 8, that becomes my come point. I back the come bet with $25 in free odds and make another come bet. If the next roll is 4, I back that come point with $15 in free odds, and wait for my results.

If the next roll is a 6, I collect $5 on my come bet and $30 in free odds, and have my wagers on that come point returned to me. My pass line bet and second come bet remain active. I'll then may choose to make another come bet to get back up to three working numbers.

This is not a system to play with a short bankroll. Note that in this sequence, once I have three points and the free odds working, I have $75 on the table. A single 7 would wipe out the entire $75. The player not only needs to have bankroll sufficient to withstand that $75 loss, the bankroll must be big enough to build up to three pass or come wagers plus odds a second time, and a third, and maybe even a fourth. Truth be told, I like to have at least $500 for the session with me before I'll play this system at a $5 table.

A player who walks up to a $5 minimum table with $100 in his pocket can't afford this system. As good a percentage play as it is, the system carries too great a danger of going broke quickly for a short-bankrolled player. So what's a player on a budget to do? That's addressed in the next answer.

2. **A short-bankrolled player who wants three numbers working but can't afford take free odds faces the lowest house edge by:**

    C. Making a pass or don't pass bet, followed by two come or don't come bets, even without the free odds

The best percentage play remains pass and come, at 1.41 percent, or don't pass and don't come, at 1.4 percent. At a $5 minimum table, with three numbers working, your risk drops to $15 that could be wiped out at one time by a 7. That makes this a system that a player with a smaller bankroll can play.

What about a player with a medium-sized bankroll, someone who brings $200 to a $5 table and plans to play for only an hour or so? Should he bump his pass and come bets up to $10? A reader once asked me that question, and I suggested that he leave his bets at the table minimum, and if he was comfortable betting a little more, to put the extra wagers into free odds instead. Since there is no house edge on the free odds, that decreases the overall house edge while giving the player the potential for larger wins.

I have a hard and fast rule: Until I'm betting maximum odds, my other bets stay minimum.

By the way, if you're of a temperament that can take standing at the table, having many rolls with no bet decided and only one number working, one pass or don't pass bet backed with odds is a better percentage play than skipping the odds while playing pass or don't pass followed by a couple of come or don't come bets. By sticking to one bet plus odds, you still can lower the house edge to 0.8 percent or less without putting the big bucks on the table.

3. Opening with a pass bet, then placing 6 and 8 (or only one of them, if the other is the point):

    B. Gives the player the two point numbers most likely to win

Rolling two six-sided dice yields 36 possible combinations. Six of those combinations total 7, more than for any other number. But 7 is a loser after a point has been established on the pass line, and it's always a loser for any place bet. There are five combinations that total 6 and five that total 8, making those two numbers the next most likely to roll after 7. For that reason, many players like to make sure they have the 6 and 8 working.

Starting with a pass bet and following it with place bets on 6 and 8 is not a bad system. In fact, when I'm short-bankrolled, it's one I sometimes use myself. It leaves you with a pass bet that bucks a 1.41 percent house edge, along with the two best place bets, each with a house edge of 1.52 percent. A pass bet followed by two come bets, even without free odds, is a better percentage system, but there is some comfort in having the 6 and 8 working.

Remember to make the place bets on 6 and 8 in multiples of $6 so the house can pay you at 7-6 odds.

4. Waiting to bet until the shooter makes a pass or two, or at least rolls a few numbers without rolling a 7:

B. Reduces the player's exposure to the house edge

The house's mathematical edge doesn't change just because you're sitting out a few rolls, but as long as you're just watching, that house edge doesn't work against you.

Frank Scoblete, in his books *Forever Craps* and *Beat the Craps out of the Casino*, describes one way to do this with his Five Count system. Once, when Frank and I were giving seminars together at the Golden Nugget in Las Vegas, Frank even delighted a couple of the folks who came to hear us by having a hot roll across Fremont Street at the Horseshoe. The guys were playing the Five Count, and Frank made the night a winner for them.

You'll have to read Frank's books to get the details on the Five Count, but I'll tell you where I think the player gains by using it or any other system that calls for watching and waiting. Basically, it extends play. If you're betting on every comeout, and things aren't going well, you go through your session bankroll fairly quickly. But if you're sitting out rolls, the house edge isn't constantly grinding against your bankroll. Maybe you miss a few wins, but you also miss some losses. Maybe instead of being done in half an hour, this delayed gratification extends your play to an hour or more. And if you're really lucky, in this extra time at the table, you'll catch a hot roll. The hot roll might not come, but at least you've extended your play and had a little fun without the night turning more costly.

Nothing can ensure that you're betting at a hot table. Hot tables do not necessarily stay hot, and cold tables do not necessarily stay cold. If several shooters in a row have had good rolls, the best you can say is that the table has been hot. Past success does not indicate future outcomes.

Now, most craps players believe in hot tables and cold tables. In fact, other players often have told me there's something mystic about a hot table that transcends the odds.

When I write that in the long run, the house percentage will catch up to everyone, that you can't beat a game with a fixed mathematical edge by using systems and money management techniques, I get letters. One fellow wants to sell his system. Another, after a column on the late Peter Griffin, accused me of being "brainwashed by that mathematician."

Games with a fixed mathematical edge in favor of the house—nearly all casino games—are said to have a negative expectation for the player. That's shorthand for saying that in the long run nearly all players will lose money. Craps is a game with a negative expectation. The 1.41 percent house edge on the pass line gives the player a reasonable chance to win at any one session, but in the long run the house will be the winner.

Still, enough players tell me that you can make money at craps by spotting hot tables that I decided to try a little experiment. One well-known system is to chart tables, watch until the shooter has made two passes in a row, then jump in.

No one has ever been able to explain just why such a table should stay hot. The dice don't know how many passes have been made.

But players like a hot table, and, more importantly, like to believe in hot tables, so I ran a little check. Actually, it was more of a big check—it took nearly a year. Whenever I was in a casino, I stopped by a craps table, waited until I saw two consecutive passes, then tracked the result of the next decision. And I also waited until there were two and consecutive don't passes and tracked the next result of that sequence. I charted until I had 1,000 trials each way—not as good a sample as a million-hand computer run even though it was a lot more time-consuming, but it consisted of real-world results.

The test covered craps tables at Hollywood in Aurora, Illinois; Grand Victoria in Elgin, Illinois; Harrah's and Empress in Joliet, Illinois; Harrah's and Hollywood in Tunica County, Mississippi, and Tropicana, MGM Grand, Excalibur, Bally's, Harrah's, Treasure Island, Riviera, Stardust, Circus Circus, Rio, Palace Station, Four Queens, Lady Luck, Fitzgerald's, Plaza and Horseshoe in Las Vegas.

The result: Pass bettors won 489 wagers and lost 511 on the next sequence after two consecutive wins. That's close enough to the mathematical expectation of 493 wins and 507 losses that we can say the percentages held up in this trial.

The more trials, the closer you'll come to the expected percentages, and 1,000 trials is really too short a test to be statistically significant. Still, there was nothing here to indicate that hot tables stay hot.

Looking at the results on the two-pass trial the other way, there's little to encourage don't pass bettors either. Among the 1,000 rolls, the number 12 came up 37 times, meaning that of the 511 losses for pass bettors, the don't players only pushed rather than won on 37 of them. That left don't bettors with 474 wins and 493 losses.

The expectation for 967 decisions would be that don't bettors would win 476 times. On the average, 12 will show 31 times per 1,000 come-out rolls. The resulting few extra pushes left don't bettors slightly behind expectation. Again, the difference is not statistically significant.

Likewise, trials starting with two don't passes showed no particular advantage to a table charter. The dice passed 496 times in those 1,000 trials—just three more passes than the expected average. There were only 28 rolls of 12 on this test, so don't players won 476 bets and lost 496, slightly below their expectation of 479 wins per 972 trials.

Not all trials of this length will work out quite so neatly. Notice that in both tests, pass bettors lost more often than they won, and so did don't pass bettors. That's not guaranteed to happen in every 1,000-trial run. There often will be some winners in tests that short.

In fact, in a 1996 edition of the newsletter the *Intelligent Gambler*, put out sporadically by software distributor ConJelCo, CrapSim programmer Ken Elliott quoted Bernie Luger's calculation that it would take 91,000 rolls for a pass bettor to be 99 percent certain of being a lifetime loser.

And, as Elliott notes, that one player in a hundred who has won more pass bets than he's lost in that time will never believe that craps is a negative expectation game.

5. A pass-line bettor who hedges by betting on any craps on the comeout roll:

   A. Gives a little extra edge to the house

Let's say that on the comeout roll, I bet $5 on the pass line, and hedge my bet by also betting $1 on any craps.

The strength of the system is that the craps rolls that would make me a loser if my only bet was on the pass line now make me a winner instead. If the shooter rolls a 7 or 11, I win $5 on the pass line and lose on any craps for a net profit of $4. If any craps—2, 3 or 12—turns up, I lose my $5 bet on the pass line, but my any craps bet, paid at 7-1 odds, brings me $7 in winnings, leaving me a net profit of $2.

Pretty neat, huh? If one bet loses, the other bet wins. Either way, I wind up with a profit for the roll.

But hold on a minute while we check out the weaknesses of the system. For starters, the true odds of rolling any craps are 8-1, but the bet pays only 7-1.

That means the hedge bettor is protecting a bet with a low house edge of 1.41 percent by making a bad bet with a house edge of 11.1 percent.

Not only that, hedging by making an any craps bet detracts from the best part of the pass-line bet—-the comeout roll. Of the 36 possible combinations of two dice, eight win on the comeout: six ways to roll 7 and two ways to roll 11. Only four combinations lose on the comeout: one way to roll 2, two ways to roll 3 and one way to roll 12.

In a perfect sequence of 36 comeout rolls in which each possible combination comes up once, a $5 pass bettor would win eight times, taking in $40, and lose four times, dropping $20, for net winnings of $20. On the other 24 rolls, a point would be established and the pass bet would be alive.

In the same sequence, a hedge bettor with $5 on the pass line and $1 on any craps also would win eight pass bets and lose for a net $20 in winnings. He'd also win four any craps bets, taking in $28, but lose 32 times, dropping $32. That leaves a net $4 in losses on any craps and cuts the player's profits on the come-out combination to $16.

By hedging his bets, the player has cost himself 20 percent of his profit.

Thanks, but no thanks.

6. A pass-line bettor who hedges by betting on any 7 after a point has been established:

A. Gives a little extra edge to the house

Let's say that I bet $5 on the pass line, and after the shooter rolls a point number, I hedge my bet by also betting $1 on any 7.

The strength of this play parallels hedging with any craps on the comeout. Here, if the shooter repeats the point number before the next 7, I win my $5 pass line bet and lose my $1 bet on any 7 for a net profit of $4. When I lose my $5 pass line bet, I win on any 7, and get a 4-1 payoff, and that $4 win limits my overall loss to just $1.

The problem is that the weaknesses here are even bigger than those of hedging with any craps on the comeout. Like any craps, any 7 is a poor bet, with a house edge of 16.67 percent. Trying to protect a good bet such as the pass line by adding a poor bet such as any of the one-roll propositions is a chip-wasting system.

At least with the any craps hedge, it's one roll and done. Hedge players use any craps on the comeout, but not many will continue to make any craps bets after a point is established. Once there's a point, craps rolls are neutral; they don't affect wins or losses on the pass line and there's no incentive to hedge against them. But players who hedge after there's a point could wind up making several any 7 wagers before the pass bet is decided. If the point number is a 6, for example, and the shooter rolls a 9, the pass-line wager remains alive but the any 7 bet loses. A player who wants to keep hedging has to make another any 7 bet, and might just have to make another . . . and another . . . and another.

To show the Hedge 7 at its best, let's assume the point is 4. As with the 10, there are only three ways to roll a 4, leaving the pass player at his most vulnerable. In a perfect sequence of 36 rolls, the $5 pass bettor will win on 4 three times, collecting $15, but lose six times, dropping $30 for a net loss of $15.

That's not an inviting scenario, but it's even worse for the Hedge 7 player. He still loses a net of $15 on the pass line. His any 7 bet wins six times for $24 in winnings, but loses 30 times for $30 in losses. That's a net loss of $6 on any 7, pushing overall losses up to $21 for the sequence.

The Hedge 7 is every bit as bad with other point numbers. With 5 or 9 as the point in our perfect sequence, the pass player wins his line bet four times for a gain of $20 on the line and loses six times to drop $30, for net losses of $10. The hedge player who also wagers on any 7 still adds $6 in losses, for a total of $16 in losses. And if the point number is 6 or 8—the second most commonly rolled numbers after 7—the player wins five times to gain $25 on the line and loses six times to drop $30 for $5 in net losses. Adding $6 in losses on any 7 more than doubles the player's total loss, bringing it to $11.

So it goes with hedges and combinations. With each additional bet, the player not only gains that wager's strengths, he also absorbs its weaknesses. And with one-roll propositions such as any craps and any 7, the weaknesses can be considerable indeed.

7. **Betting $26 across or $27 across gives the player:**
   C. Bets on every place number except the point on the pass line

Here's the way it works. Let's say I have $5 on the pass line, and the shooter rolls a 6 on the comeout, making that the point. I then put chips on the layout, and tell the dealer, 26 across. The dealer then will give me $5 place bets on 4, 5, 9 and 10 and a $6 bet on 8. (Remember, we place 6 or 8 in $6 increments so the house can pay us at 7-6 odds.) That's a total of $26.

If neither 6 nor 8 is the point, then I'd ask for 27 across, because I have to bet an extra dollar to make sure both the 6 and 8 wagers are in multiples of $6.

Now, I don't really make this bet, regardless of whether it's $26 across or $27 across. The house edge on place bets on 5 and 9 is 4 percent, and the house edge on 4 and 10 is 6.67 percent.

As far as I'm concerned, across the board is across the line I draw for acceptable house edges. If I'm inclined to bet place numbers, I'll stick to 6 and 8 with their house edge of 1.52 percent.

8.   Darby's Field, also known as the dinner bet:
   B.   Will win more often than it loses.

It's easy to come up with systems that will win more often than they lose. Cover enough numbers and you win more often than you lose. The problem is that you're going to go broke doing it. That's because when you lose, the losses are big enough to negate several wins.

Take the dinner bet. Please.

Supposedly, this combination of bets got its nickname from players in Las Vegas who would make it at dinnertime. Win just one bet, take the rest down and use the winnings to buy dinner— or at least a cheap buffet.

You start by betting $5 on the field. Then you add a $5 place bet on 5 and a $6 place bet on 6. That gives you nine winning numbers—2, 3, 4, 9, 10, 11 and 12 on the field, plus your place bets on 5 and 6. The only losing rolls are 7 and 8. There are six ways to roll 7 and five ways to roll 8, so in 36 possible rolls of the dice, there are only 11 losers. The other 25 rolls are winners.

You can almost hear the prime rib mooing, right?

Well, it's not quite that simple. For one thing, you're really hoping one of the field numbers comes in so you win that bet and can take down the place bets without losing anything. If, instead, one your place bets is the winner, most of the win is offset by losing the field bet. When that happens, your win is only $2, and dinner is going to be mighty skimpy. Popcorn, anyone?

Your biggest potential win is when the roll is 2 or 12. That's at least a 2-1 payoff, and in some casinos the 12 in the field pays 3-1. With either a $10 or $15 win, you can buy a pretty nice casino dinner. Problem is, 2 shows up only once per 36 rolls, and so does 12. Meanwhile, if the roll is 7 or 8, you lose all three bets for a total of $16 in losses.

Let's once again start with a perfect sequence of 36 rolls in which each combination comes up once. We bet $16 on each roll, so our total risk is $576.

On each of the five times the roll is 6, you win $7 on that place bet, but lose $5 in the field. Net win is $2 for each time this happens, or a total of $10 for the 36-roll sequence.

On each of the four times the roll is 5, you also win $7 on the place bet but lose $5 in the field. Net win is $2 per roll, or a total of $8 for the sequence.

On each of the 14 times the field wins with a roll of 3, 4, 9, 10 or 11, you win $5 in the field and take down your place bets with no losses. That's a profit of $5 per roll, or a total of $70 for the sequence. Even a $5 win makes this more of a breakfast buffet bet than a dinner bet, but this system was named in a time of lower prices.

On the one time the field wins with a roll of 2, you win $10. In many Las Vegas coffee shops, you now can afford a steak dinner.

On the one time the field wins with a roll of 12, you either win $10 if the 12 pays 2-1 or $15 if the payoff is 3-1. Have a glass of wine with that steak.

So with totals of $10 in winnings on rolls of 6, $8 on the 5s, $70 on field wins that pay even money, $10 on the 2 and either $10 or $15 on the 12, our total profit on winning rolls is either $108 or $113.

Now for the losses.

On the six times the roll is 7, we lose both place bets and the field bet. That's $16 in losses per 7, or $96 for the sequence.

On the five times the roll is 8, we lose the field bet, but we take down the two place bets. That limits our losses to $5 per 8, or $40 for the sequence.

With $96 in losses on 7 and $40 in losses on 8, we drop a total of $136 on losing rolls. Subtract the wins, and overall, we lose $28 for the entire sequence if the field 12 pays 2-1, or $23 if the 12 pays 3-1.

The house edge on the dinner bet works out to 3.99 percent if the house offers the better version of the field, or 4.86 percent on the lesser version. Either way, it's not so much a dinner bet as it's a lose your lunch bet.

9. Combination bets give the player:

  C. All the strengths and all the weaknesses in each bet in the combination

The dinner bet described above is not detailed here because it's an important system. It's designed as a hit-and-run one-roll play, and it's here to serve as an example of what happens when you try to put a combination bet together. But players, in trying to find a perfectly balanced combination, devise all kinds of systems. Every player needs to realize that for every hole you plug up by adding a bet to the combination, you open yet another hole. Sometimes the hole is as simple and gaping as the dinner bet problem that a 7 means losses on the field and the place bets all at once. Sometimes it's slightly less obvious, such as the Hedge 7 problem that any 7 is a one-roll bet and the player could lose several any 7 wagers before the pass line bet is decided.

In any case, combination bets can't diminish the house edge. The house's mathematical edge remains in effect for every piece of the combination, no matter what you do.

Your best defense is simply to stick with the best bets at the table. If you're going to use combinations, or if you simply want to have several numbers working at once, use only the wagers with low house edges. Stick to pass and don't pass, come and don't come, the free odds, and place wagers on 6 and 8, and you'll be cutting the house edge as far as it can go.

10. Money management systems:

  B. Can help the player extend play

Money management systems have no effect on the house edge, and they can't make you a winner in the long run. If you're betting any 7, in the long run you're going to lose $16.67 for every $100 you bet, and it doesn't matter whether you bet a flat $1 every time, or double up your bet after losses, or add a unit after each win, or any other money management scheme you can come up with.

But money management can help you stay in the game longer if it involves making bets of a sensible size given your bankroll and, yes, even sitting out a few rolls, as in the Frank Scoblete Five Count system mentioned earlier in this chapter.

Not all systems will help you. In fact, some schemes are downright dangerous. Sooner or later nearly every player thinks about doubling his bet after losses. If I start with a $5 bet on the pass line and lose, I bet $10. Then if I win, I show a $5 overall profit for the sequence. If I lose at $10, I double to $20, and if I lose at $20, I double to $40. Whenever a win finally comes, it wipes out all my previous losses and leaves me with a $5 profit overall.

That's a very common, and very old system called a Martingale. The problem is that the bets get very large, very quickly and run up against the maximum bets posted at the tables.

If a player could use the Martingale indefinitely, he would eventually show a profit every time. He would just keep doubling up until he wins. It's infallible—except that it doesn't work that way in the real world. Casinos foil the Martingale by placing limits on wagers at each table. At a table with a $5 minimum and a $500 maximum, a Martingale player on a losing streak could bet $5, $10, $20, $40, $80, $160, $320, but the next bet in the sequence would be $640. So with seven losses in a row, the Martingale player is unable to place a bet large enough to recoup his losses. Even if you could get the bet down, would you really want to be risking $640 in an attempt to show a $5 profit?

Seven-loss sequences happen often enough that a player who attempts to use a Martingale will lose money in the long run.

That brings me to a system I once received in the mail from a fellow who insisted he had found a way to get a mathematical edge on craps. It was a modified Martingale that involved betting a specified percentage of previous losses, rather than doubling up after each loss, and was applied to the pass-line bet in craps. The author said he'd found the exact percentage that turned craps into a positive expectation game. In a computer run of 1 million decisions, the system showed profits of $11,265.

So far, so good. But, as you might expect, there were problems. The starting point for all betting sequences was a pass wager of $1. And the author said the largest bet required was a little more than $10,000, and that $10,000 bets "can be made in Las Vegas without getting permission first."

But those $10,000 wagers can't be made at $1 tables—maximums ranging from $50 to $500 are more typical. And note that he said his largest wagers were more than $10,000. The sheet he sent along, which showed the largest bet for each set of 10,000 decisions, showed two bets exceeding $10,000. (There may have been more oversized bets that just weren't the largest in those sequences.) Not only could he not get these bets down at $1 tables, he couldn't get them down anywhere without permission from the pit.

The largest bet shown, $11,298, exceeded all winnings from the million-trial run. Not only does a player have to be well financed to even attempt this method, if he can't get this bet down, the system loses and table limits have done their job.

The bottom line is that without using bets that couldn't be made in the real world, the system lost money over the course of the trial. Even if it hadn't, would you, as a $1 bettor at the start, really want to have more than $11,000 on the table in an attempt to squeeze out a profit?

There are plenty of other money management systems out there that try to beat the game through varying the size of your bets. Some players like betting progressions, in which they bet more after wins and scale back after losses. For example, if you win a $5 bet, advance to $7 after a win, $10 after a second win and $15 after a third. After the $15 bet, go back to $5, win or lose. A simple progression such as that is fun, easy and doesn't carry the dangers of bankruptcy the Martingale brings . . . but it can't overcome the house edge in the long run.

The best money management system is the one that ensures that you walk out of the casino without losing more than you can afford.

Never play with money you can't afford to lose: Winning is fun, but losses are inevitable in any casino game. When the losses come, make sure you're not losing money you need for rent, mortgage or groceries.

Never borrow money to gamble: I once received a phone call from a woman who had been playing slot machines and lost $8,000 of money she'd borrowed against a credit card. She thought something was wrong with the game. What was wrong was her management of her money. She was stuck paying off that bill at credit card interest rates. Don't make that mistake.

Stay within your playing budget for the day: Before you leave home, decide how much money you can afford to gamble, and don't go beyond that. Treat the trip to the casino as a day's entertainment, and your gambling money as your entertainment budget. If you wouldn't find it at all entertaining to lose a couple of hundred dollars, don't bring that much money.

Don't overbet your bankroll: As we discussed in Answer No. 1 in this section, a player who walks up a $5 table with $100 in his pocket can't afford to bet on the pass line and follow with two come bets, all backed with free odds. One 7 that wipes out three bets plus odds at once could eat much of that bankroll. Short-bankrolled players have to use cheaper methods of play, whether it's skipping the odds or just making a place bet on 6 or heading off to play some quarter video poker. Overbetting your bankroll makes for a short day.

Don't chase losses: Sometimes players who have lost a good chunk of money start increasing bets, or chasing wild long shots, trying to win it all back. The most likely result of all that is that they lose even more. Set a loss limit for yourself, and if you reach that limit, understand that the money is gone, and it's time for you to go, too. Don't compound your losses.

Money management alone can't beat the games or overcome the house edge. But managing your money wisely and sticking to limits can help extend your stay in the casino and make it more fun without undue damage to your bankroll.

Pass 10:
The Readers Write

One of the things I do on a regular basis in my newspaper column is to answer questions from readers. The following are 10 questions on craps readers sent me. No multiple choices here; see if you can figure out the answers after having read the previous chapters of the book:

1. My local casino just went to 100x odds at the craps tables, and I heard that pass bettors can lower the house edge to two-hundredths of a percent. Most gaming writers I've read say that blackjack is the best game for the player. With 100x odds at craps, does that change?

2. I heard that a casino in Las Vegas was paying 33-1 on 12 instead of the usual 30-1. I know the 12 is a bet to avoid, but with that payoff is it worth making?

3. Every book I've read on craps lists the house edge on the pass-and-odds combination as 0.8 percent. Why isn't it 0.7 percent? If I make a $5 pass bet and back it with $5 in odds, the house edge of 1.41 percent on the line is balanced off by the zero percent odds wager. So shouldn't the house edge on the combination just be the 1.41 percent divided by two?

4. You repeatedly list the house edge on the pass line as 1.41 percent. When I calculate it, I come up with something more like 2.8 percent. Could you show me how the house edge on the pass line is calculated?

5. I recently got back from a week in Las Vegas, where I heard about Crapless Craps being played at the Stratosphere.

I checked out this craps variation and here's what I found. It's just like regular craps except there's no don't pass line—if you roll 2, 3, 11 or 12 on the comeout roll, that's your point. Only 7 wins on the comeout. So they give you a chance to make your point on 2, 3 or 12, which otherwise would be an instant loser. But the catch is they take away the 11.

Free odds wagers at true odds are offered on these new points just like the other numbers. This boosts the house advantage from 1.414 percent to 5.382 percent.

Also, if the table is cold, where do you go? Don't pass is gone. What do you think?

6. I have a strange question. Recently I bought four canceled Las Vegas craps dice. However, I also noticed that the 6 face is etched very lightly with a word. Each die has a different word. RAFT is one, and I can't recall the others. What does this mean?

7. How should a limited session bankroll affect taking odds in a 3x, 4x, 5x odds situation? Since I usually have a limited bankroll, I often pretend I'm in a single- or double-odds game so that I can make a come bet or two with odds in addition to my pass-line bet with odds and still keep under budget for the shoot. Shepherding only one number (even a 6 with 5x odds) is pretty boring and I never make proposition bets. Any comments?

8. Why would anybody make pass or come bets instead of place bets on 6 or 8? If you bet $30 on the pass line and the shooter makes a point of 6, what do you win? Thirty dollars. If I place the 6 for $30, what do I win? THIRTY-FIVE DOLLARS! Aren't you just giving away your money with the pass bet instead?

9. I was staying recently at a casino hotel where the craps tables offered 10x odds. I was betting pretty big—a $10 pass bet followed by two $10 come bets, each backed with $100 in odds. So I had $330 on the table at any one time. But at the end of the stay, when I asked a host to comp my room and food, he wouldn't do it!

10. If there is no house edge on the free odds, why do casinos offer them? Aren't they in the business to make money?

Pass No. 10:
The Readers Write
Answers

1. **My local casino just went to 100x odds at the craps tables, and I heard that pass bettors can lower the house edge to two-hundredths of a percent. Most gaming writers I've read say that blackjack is the best game for the player. With 100x odds at craps, does that change?**

    ANSWER: It depends on your bankroll and your blackjack skill level. Card counters can get an edge on blackjack, while there is no way to entirely eliminate the house edge at craps.

    Very few blackjack players count cards, so let's step down a level. Basic strategy players can cut the house edge in blackjack to about 0.5 percent, plus or minus a couple of tenths of a percent depending on house rules. That means that on average they lose about 50 cents of every $100 they wager.

    A craps player betting the pass line faces a house edge of 1.41 percent. If the pass bet is backed with single odds, the house edge drops to 0.8 percent, and double odds drops it to 0.6 percent. By the time you get to 100x odds, the house edge on the pass/odds combination is down to 0.021 percent, meaning the player loses an average of just over 2 cents per $100 wagered.

    So far, so good, and it looks like the craps player is getting the better end of the stick. But to get that deal, the craps player has to bet far more money than the blackjack player.

    Let's say you walk into a casino with $5 minimum bets at blackjack, and $5 minimum pass line bets at craps. If you know basic strategy, you can narrow the house edge at blackjack to 0.5 percent even while making $5 minimum bets. At the craps table, if you simply make $5 pass bets, the house edge stays at 1.41 percent, nearly three times that faced by the blackjack basic strategy player.

To narrow the house edge to 0.6 percent, approximating the blackjack edge, you have to back that pass bet with double odds, meaning a total wager of $15 whenever a point number is established.

To get a similar break on the house edge, the craps player has to bet about three times as much money as the blackjack player.

And to take full advantage of 100x odds and cut the house edge to next to nothing, that $5 pass bet has to be backed by $500 in free odds. Low house edge or not, this is not a play for the faint of heart or the short of bankroll.

Let's go down one more step. What about players who don't take the time to study basic strategy in blackjack? Casinos figure the house edge against an average blackjack player is about 2 percent to 2.5 percent. Some weak players face house edges of double that or more. For those players, the pass line bet alone, even without the free odds, is a better percentage bet than blackjack.

So if we're to judge the games by house edge alone, blackjack is a better game for card counters or basic strategy players with low to moderate bankrolls. If enough odds are offered, craps yields a lower house edge for non-card counters with big bankrolls or players who don't use basic strategy in blackjack.

2. I heard that a casino in Las Vegas was paying 33-1 on 12 instead of the usual 30-1. I know the 12 is a bet to avoid, but with that payoff is it worth making?

ANSWER: When the Resort at Summerlin north of Las Vegas opened in the fall of 1999, one-roll propositions on 2 or 12 paid 33-to-1, leaving a house edge of 5.6 percent. Resort also paid 16-1 on 3 or 11, also yielding a house edge of 5.6 percent.

Other one-roll wagers with increased payoffs and reduced

house edges were any 7, which paid 4.5-to-1 for an edge of 8.3 percent, and any craps, which paid 7.5-to-1 for a house edge of 5.6 percent.

The hardways were also improved, with a hard 4 or 10 paying 7.5-to-1, for a house edge of 5.6 percent, and hard 6 or 8 paying 9.5-1, for a house edge of 4.5 percent.

These wagers still aren't in the ballpark with pass or come (1.41 percent house edge), don't pass or don't come (1.4 percent) or place bets on 6 or 8 (1.52 percent). They're better than the usual deal on those propositions, but they're still not good bets.

3. **Every book I've read on craps lists the house edge on the pass-and-odds combination as 0.8 percent. Why isn't it 0.7 percent? If I make a $5 pass bet and back it with $5 in odds, the house edge of 1.41 percent on the line is balanced off by the zero percent odds wager. So shouldn't the house edge on the combination just be the 1.41 percent divided by two?**

ANSWER: One-third of all pass-line bets are decided on the comeout roll, before the player is allowed to make an odds wager. Those odds-less decisions account for 45 percent of our pass-line wins and 22 percent of our losses.

The free odds wager, paid at true odds and carrying no house edge, offsets the house edge on our line bet only on the two-thirds of betting sequences in which a point number is established. Since that bet is not on the table for every decision, it can't halve the house edge on a pass-single odds combination. Instead, it cuts the house edge to 0.8 percent with single odds and 0.6 percent with double odds.

4. **You repeatedly list the house edge on the pass line as 1.41 percent. When I calculate it, I come up with something more like 2.8 percent. Could you show me how the house edge on the pass line is calculated?**

ANSWER: There are 36 possible two-dice combinations, so we start with perfect sequences of 36 rolls in which each possible combination turns up once. Just so that everything comes out in whole numbers, I'm going to use 55 perfect sequences of 36 rolls, or 1,980 comeout rolls.

On average, we will get the following results:

Win on the comeout: 330 7s and 110 11s.

Lose on the comeout: 110 3s, 55 2s and 55 12s.

Establish a point: 275 6s, 275 8s, 220 5s, 220 9s, 165 4s and 165 10s.

Now let's imagine we bet $1 on the pass line for each comeout. Each winning bet brings us a $2 return—the $1 we wagered plus $1 in winnings.

We win on the comeout 440 times for a $880 return.

We lose on the comeout 220 times for zero return.

That leaves the point numbers. To start with, let's group the 6s and 8s together since the odds are the same. We have 550 6s and 8s. In a perfect sequence of 36 rolls, there are six 7s, five 5s and five 8s. The odds are 6-5 against us winning when either of these numbers is the point.

On average, we win five times and lose six in each 11 trials. With 550 trials, we have 50 groups of 11. That will give us 250 wins and 300 losses. At a $2 return for each win, our return is $500.

On our 440 5s and 9s, the odds against us are 3-2. Of each group of five bets, we will win two and lose three. In 440 trials, there are 88 groups of five. Multiply 88 by 2 wins per group, and our total is 176 wins and 264 losses. Those 176 wins give us a $352 return.

On our 330 4s and 10s, the odds against us are 2-1. Of each group of three bets, we will win one and lose two. There are 110 groups of three, so we win 110 bets and lose 220 for a return of $220.

That leaves our returns as follows: $880 on 7s and 11s; $500 on 6s and 8s; $352 on 5s and 9s, and $220 on 4s and 10s.

Add that all up, and our total return is $1,952. Subtract that from our total wager of $1,980, and we see the house has kept $28. Divide the $28 house profit by the $1,980 in wagers, and we get 0.0141, or 1.41 percent. That's the house edge.

We can do the same thing on the don't pass side, and our returns for our $1,980 in wagers are as follows:

Don't pass wins or pushes on the comeout: $220 on the 110 3s, $110 on the 55 2s and $55 on the 55 12s. (We get only $1 back for each 12 because the wager is a push, and just our bet is returned.)

Don't pass loses on the comeout: We get no return on the 330 7s and 110 11s

Point number established: We get a $600 return on the 300 times of 550 trials the shooter 7s out with a point 6 or point 8. We get $528 on the 264 times of 440 trials the shooter 7s out with a point 5 or 9. And we get $440 on the 220 times of 330 trials the shooter 7s out with a point 4 or 10.

Add that up, and our total return is $1,953—or $1 better than the pass bettor does with the same sequence. The house wins $27. Divide by $1,980 in total wagers and you get a house edge of 1.36 percent. Most gambling writers use 1.4 percent instead because we assume the bettor is not going to take down his wager after pushing on 12. Letting the house edge work against that wager until there's a decision brings the total up to 1.4 percent.

5. **I recently got back from a week in Las Vegas, where I heard about Crapless Craps being played at the Stratosphere.**

    I checked out this craps variation and here's what I found. It's just like regular craps except there's no don't pass line—if you roll 2, 3, 11 or 12 on the comeout roll, that's your point. Only 7 wins on the comeout. So they give you a chance to make your point on 2, 3 or 12, which otherwise would be an instant loser. But the catch is they take away the 11.

    Free odds wagers at true odds are offered on these new points just like the other numbers. This boosts the house advantage from 1.414 percent to 5.382 percent.

    Also, if the table is cold, where do you go? Don't pass is gone. What do you think? I'll stick to regular craps.

ANSWER: Crapless Craps was introduced at Bob Stupak's Vegas World, which used to sit on the site from which the Stratosphere Tower now rises. The game sounds like a great deal until you take a hard look. What could be better than never losing on the comeout?

The problem is that the tradeoffs are too big. Your calculations on crapless craps are correct—the house edge is almost quadruple that in the normal game. Losing the 11 as an automatic winner on the comeout is tough enough, but it gets worse. Instead of winning on the comeout, that 11 becomes a poor point number, one that pass bettors lose three times for every one they win.

And for what gain? The 2, 3 and 12 also are poor point numbers. Even though you don't lose on the comeout, you'll still lose an average of six times for every seven times the point is 2 or 12, and three of four times the point is 3. A pass line bet pays only even money on a 6-1 shot on 2 or 12 and a 3-1 shot on 3.

And, as you note, there is no don't pass bet in Crapless Craps. And since don't pass is a marginally better percentage bet than pass, with a house advantage of 1.4 percent, that means one of the best bets around is gone.

Unlike regular craps, the crapless version adds place bets on 2, 3, 11 and 12. Winners on 2 or 12 pay 11-2, and winners on 3 or 11 pay 11-4. House edges are 7.14 percent to place 2 or 12 or 6.25 percent on 3 and 11.

Stick to regular craps. The price you pay to go crapless is too high.

6. **I have a strange question. Recently I bought four canceled Las Vegas craps dice. However, I also noticed that the 6 face is etched very lightly with a word. Each die has a different word. RAFT is one, and I can't recall the others. What does this mean?**

    ANSWER: A supervisor scratches each craps die with his initials or name to signify they belong in play at that table. It's a little protection against someone making a switch and bringing dishonest dice into play. At the end of that supervisor's shift, the dice are canceled.

7. **How should a limited session bankroll affect taking odds in a 3x, 4x, 5x odds situation? Since I usually have a limited bankroll, I often pretend I'm in a single- or double-odds game so that I can make a come bet or two with odds in addition to my pass-line bet with odds and still keep under budget for the shoot. Shepherding only one number (even a 6 with 5x odds) is pretty boring and I never make proposition bets. Any comments?**

   ANSWER: Pretending it's a single- or double-odds game is a perfectly reasonable way to stretch your bankroll. Taking maximum odds available is still the best percentage bet, but if your goal is to keep playing, to have a reasonable shot to win and not risk tapping out on one bad roll, the short-bankrolled player sometimes must compromise on the amount of odds he takes.

8. **Why would anybody make pass or come bets instead of place bets on 6 or 8? If you bet $30 on the pass line and the shooter makes a point of 6, what do you win? Thirty dollars. If I place the 6 for $30, what do I win? THIRTY-FIVE DOL-LARS! Aren't you just giving away your money with the pass bet instead?**

   ANSWER: You miss the point that the best part of a pass or come bet is before a point is established. If I'm betting $30 on the comeout roll and the shooter rolls a 7 or 11, what do I win? Thirty dollars. What do you win? Zero. Zip. Nada. On the comeout, I have eight ways to win and only four ways to lose. If you're like most place bettors, you don't even have your bet working on a comeout roll, so while I'm making money, you're on the side-lines. And if you do have your place bet on 6 working on the comeout, you have the same six ways to lose and five ways to win that you always do. On that roll, I'm the favorite and you're the underdog, and that more than offsets any advantage your place bet may have after a point is established.

9. **I was staying recently at a casino hotel where the craps tables offered 10x odds. I was betting pretty big—a $10 pass bet followed by two $10 come bets, each backed with $100 in odds. So I had $330 on the table at any one time. But at the end of the stay, when I asked a host to comp my room and food, he wouldn't do it!**

ANSWER: Many casinos don't include the free odds in calculating a player's average bet. There is no house advantage on the odds, so they don't expect to make any money off that portion of your bet. As far as the casino was concerned, you were a $30 bettor, and that $30 was wagered on good percentage bets. The casino will return as comps anywhere from 10 percent to 40 percent of your expected losses, but with the bets you were making, your expected average losses were only a couple of bucks per hour.

If you try different casinos, you might find one that will comp a room or perhaps some meals at your level of play. Even if you don't get the comps, you're far better off protecting your bankroll with solid bets such as the ones you were making than to waste your money over the field, hardways or one-roll propositions. At your bet level, wagers like that would get you the comps, but you'd more than pay for them with increased losses.

10. **If there is no house edge on the free odds, why do casinos offer them? Aren't they in the business to make money?**

ANSWER: Yes, of course they're in the business to make money. Their sole purpose is to show you a good enough time that you'll willingly leave some of your money behind.

The free odds don't add to the casinos' bottom line by taking your money, but they do attract players. Note that casinos who are trying for bigger craps play often try to attract players by boosting the amount of free odds available. Ten years ago, triple odds were a treat and the 10x odds being offered by the Horseshoe in Las Vegas were practically a dream. Now many markets have casinos offering 100x odds.

Bibliography

There are many excellent books on craps on the market, and it seems everyone who writes about the game has his or her own ideas on how to attack it. The following are some of the best books on the market, books that I find myself learning from every time I re-read them:

The Dice Doctor by Sam Grafstein ($14.95), published by Gambler's Book Club Press, Las Vegas, NV 89101. Web site: www.gamblersbook.com

Forever Craps ($13.95) and *Beat the Craps out of the Casino* ($9.95), both by Frank Scoblete, published by Bonus Books, 160 E. Illinois Street, Chicago, IL, 60611. Web site: www.bonus-books.com

Craps: *Take the Money and Run* by Henry Tamburin ($11.95), Research Services Unlimited, PO Box 19727, Greensboro, NC 27419. Web site: www.smartgaming.com

Other Books by John Grochowski

Autographed copies of all John's books are available on request when ordered from Running Count Press, PO Box 1488, Elmhurst, IL 60126. Running Count does not charge for shipping.

The Video Poker Answer Book ($13.95), Bonus Books, 160 E. Illinois Street, Chicago, IL, 60611. Web site: www.bonus-books.com. More than 300 answers to your questions on video poker, including how to vary your strategies to get the most when casinos change the pay tables.

The Slot Machine Answer Book ($12.95), Bonus Books. John Grochowski answers nearly 200 questions on slot machines, from their colorful history with tidbits such as how the bars and fruit symbols wound up on the slot reels, to how best to take advantage of modern bonus slots, slot clubs and tournaments.

The Casino Answer Book ($12.95), Bonus Books. In the first of the series of Answer Books, John Grochowski focuses on blackjack, video poker and roulette, with everything from how an English game called roly-poly led to the development of modern roulette, to the right times to double down at the blackjack table.

Gaming: Cruising the Casinos ($11.95), Running Count Press, PO Box 1488, Elmhurst, IL 60126. A compilation of 67 essays on casino gambling, from blackjack to baccarat and slot clubs to progressive betting.

Winning Tips for Casino Games ($4.99), Publications International, 7373 N. Cicero Avenue, Lincolnwood, IL 60646. This 144-page small-format book is a basic primer on how to play casino games.